N'

# PRACTICAL POULTRY
# KEEPING

PRACTICAL

# Poultry Keeping

*David Bland*

The Crowood Press

First published in 1996 by
The Crowood Press Ltd
Ramsbury, Marlborough
Wiltshire SN8 2HR

This impression 1998

**British Library Cataloguing in Publication Data**

A catalogue record for this book is available from the British Library

ISBN 1 86126 010 5

**Picture Credits**

All photographs supplied by Alexandra Bastedo, David M. and Barrie Bland, Brinsea Incubators, Chelwood Outdoor Feeders, Curfew Incubators, Ecostat Ltd, Lurgan Fibre Ltd, Julian Moores, Mike John, Jo Coates, *Poultry World* and SPR. Photographic technician – Dave J. Green.

All line-drawings by Debra Syme and Annette Findlay

**Acknowledgements**

Special thanks to Valerie Bland and Alexandra Bastedo for their help in reading and correcting the initial manuscript. The author also wishes to acknowledge the additional technical advice given by David Applegarth and David Spackman NDP BVSc MRCVS.

Typeset by Phoenix Typesetting, Ilkley, West Yorkshire

Printed and bound in Great Britain by
BPC Consumer Books, Aylesbury

# Contents

# Foreword

In *Practical Poultry Keeping* David Bland makes a lifetime of practical experience available to his readers. Be they hobbyists, small-scale commercial farmers or simply have an interest in the development of the poultry industry, all will benefit from this accumulated expertise.

The book will be particularly valuable to those who wish to produce eggs and poultry in a traditional and less intensive manner than that currently employed by commerce. Other books concentrate on free-range methods, but here the author gives the reader the choice of several alternatives.

**Peter Day**
Former Chief Poultry Adviser
to ADAS, MAFF, now running
his own Poultry Industry
Consultancy

# Introduction

This book has been written after forty-five years' experience of practical poultry farming and will guide the reader step by step through each of the various stages of setting up and maintaining a unit, which will not only conform to welfare legislation but will be viable, avoiding many, if not all, of the common errors so frequently encountered at the cost of the producer. Units fail mostly because of ignorance through lack of training, and the problems often experienced by the novice can result in avoidable disease, severe injury and unacceptably high levels of mortality. It may be argued by some that to take on board all EC legislation will cause an otherwise successful business to fail. I hope to show the reader in the ensuing chapters how to achieve both viability and welfare.

Many large companies embark on alternative systems of egg production without understanding the fundamental requirements of the laying bird in these new environments. I say 'new' as since the late 1960s egg production has been increasingly intensified, moving away from an environment which was and is today very problematical. With the advent of battery units, mortality was greatly reduced and several diseases associated with extensive production disappeared.

During the late 1960s and until the early 1970s there were many advisors whose academic qualifications were backed by a sound practical background, financed by the larger feed companies and supported in Britain by the Government's own National Agricultural Advisory Service (NAAS). During this period agricultural colleges were full of agricultural and poultry students, and some maintained long waiting-lists for poultry students. The overall standard of management of the farming community was very practical and knowledgeable, kept up to date by an exemplary advisory network.

Today, these same agricultural colleges, which in many cases have further expanded, attract very few, if any, students who wish to enter the field of agriculture. Instead, places are taken by those hoping for careers in the leisure business. Those highly respected advisors have long since retired and have been replaced by a much smaller band who seem unable to relate to the practical application of past systems. Now, unfortunately, advice emanates from those whose only training is in intensive environments and who fail to understand that extensive systems require different techniques, purpose-designed poultry housing, more specialized feed, hardier birds and a higher standard of management, which are all quite alien to their intensive counterparts.

# 1　Utility Breeds

## THE HISTORY OF THE SPECIES

The historical background of poultry is important because, with a better knowledge of its ancestry and background, poultry keepers are better able to understand the hens' requirements concerning most aspects of management. Armed with this knowledge, they will be able to improve the welfare of their birds on a practical basis, providing a suitable environment for them.

Domestic poultry can be traced back to when people gave up nomadic life and settled in small villages. They gathered around them all the animals that could supply their daily needs and these included chickens. There is a lot of truth in Rudyard Kipling's *Just So Stories*: the animals received, in return for sacrifice of liberty, comfort, protection and food.

Darwin's first evolution theory that all poultry orginated from one fowl, Gallus Bankiva, was in later years rejected because there were definite differences of preferred habitat and natural behaviour between types of chicken. Gallus Bankiva, although varying to some extent in natural instincts and colour, depending on the Asiatic country in which it was found, is probably responsible for much of our present-day population of poultry, especially with regard to game birds and what are commonly known as light breeds.

However, it is difficult to dispute that our present-day heavy breeds have originated from a different source; this is evident from both their character and bone formation. These long, feather-legged heavy birds known nowadays as Cochins and Brahmas came from China and are altogether distinct from any other breeds of poultry. In-depth investigation by naturalists has not been able to explain the variations between the two main species, although these differences have been acknowledged by experienced poultry breeders the world over. To this day, no Gallus has been discovered from which modern heavy breeds are derived, and to which the Cochin and Brahma can be ascribed.

*Cochin hen.*

9

*Cochin cockerel.*

# UTILITY BREEDS

There are a great many different light and heavy breeds of poultry, the majority of which owe their continued existence to the enthusiasm of show breeders and exhibitors. Out of all the breeds there are now only about eight which are of any commercial interest for the economical production of eggs. Producers for many years now have been subjected to strains of hybrids. Work on these continues in an attempt to achieve an even higher production of large eggs while at the same time reducing the amount of feed intake. Feed represents some 70 per cent of the cost of production and is therefore a major concern of breeders and producers alike.

## Rhode Island Red

Since its introduction, this has been the best and most popular of all brown-egg producing birds in Britain. The only disadvantage was that all Rhode cockerels, caponized and run on for table production, were downgraded because of the yellow pigmentation showing on skin and fat. In this country the customer has always preferred birds with white flesh and white fat, contrary to many other countries who acknowledge that yellow pigmentation stock are slightly more nutrious than white.

Today the Rhode is the major breed from which all brown-egg laying strains of hybrids are derived, the cockerels also being used with Leghorns to produce light cream eggs for many other world markets. In the 1950s it was still noted for slow feather growth which was a disadvantage to the rearer, but since then it has been improved so much that it feathers as well as any other brown-egg layer. For those wishing to breed their own stock replacement, then the Rhode Island should be the first breed to be considered provided

The importance of recognizing these two species of poultry lies in their differing characteristic habits which affect modern-day poultry keeping.

The Gallus Bankiva's background is that of a jungle bird which perched, found shelter under shrubs and hedges, made nests in deep undergrowth and was very flighty and aggressive. The Brahma and Cochin (more popularly referred to as the Shanghai), nested on the ground in clear open spaces and tended to congregate as partridges do, flocking together in the centre of open ground. When these birds commenced laying, unless some kind of coop was available they chose some heap or mound to nest on, and laid brown-coloured eggs. Bankiva, on the other hand, roosted in trees and nested in hedgerows or dense shrubs producing only pure white eggs.

*Rhode Island Red.*

it originates from a known utility line and not exhibition stock.

## Light Sussex

The Light Sussex originated from the Speckled Barn Fowl before and during Roman times, and was to be found in most European countries as far as and including Russia. It was one of the genera of early table birds reared and sold at the same time as the Dorking Fowl. The latter was produced as the Sussex in the Weald of Sussex, their main market being Horsham. The Light Sussex, not regarded by purists as a true Sussex, was probably produced by out-breeding with Cochin blood, and as a result the egg colour became tinted and its proliferation of eggs was greatly improved. At laying trials after the war the Light Sussex, although regarded as a dual-purpose breed (for meat and eggs), proved its egg-producing ability by coming third to the Leghorn,

11

*Two Light Sussex cockerels.*

with the Rhode Island coming top. Another advantage of this dual-purpose bird was that when crossed using a Rhode Island Red cockerel the progeny were sex linked. The pullet chicks are gold and the cockerel chicks yellow. Nowadays, without the advantage of caponization the cockerels are killed immediately after hatching, and used to supply the trade and charities to feed rescued birds of prey.

## Plymouth Rock

This is an American breed produced before the turn of the century with the aid of the Cochin. At present, commercial breeding stock is held and bred in Scotland by one breeder, which he crosses with Rhode Island Red males to produce an excellent free range hybrid. Both these lines originated in America, and were later sold to South Africa. They were then brought to Scotland by Mr Peter Siddons, who produced a bird known as the Black Rock which is now distributed throughout the UK. Although this particular hybrid has not proved popular to intensive egg producers because of its greater size and slightly higher feed consumption, it has proved to be the ideal free range bird, coping better than any other with the extremes of our varied climate.

## Wyandotte

The Wyandotte originated in America as the Silver Laced Wyandotte. Two of the original breeds involved in its production are the Cochin and Brahma. The feather lacing of the Silver-Laced Wyandotte came about in its original formation with the introduction of the Silver Sebright Bantam on either the Cochin or Brahma, plus the use of the Silver-Spangled Hamburgh. Some lines produced small eggs associated with the use of the Sebright in its origin, but other improved lines made it a very prolific producer of white or cream coloured eggs, sharing popularity with the other white-egg layer, the Leghorn.

The White Wyandotte is a sport of the Silver Laced which was developed in Britain before being exported back to the States, where it became an important and popular egg-producing breed. It is claimed that the White is a true British breed and is responsible in developing the White Rhode, which is now such a very important part of most of the modern-day hybrids.

It has been claimed that it produced more eggs than any other breed under cold wet conditions, which is a far cry from its present-day show counterpart. There are only one or two breeders left in Britain who still possess a true utility line. The colour of the egg has been mainly responsible for its downfall here. Its blood lines were included in the make-up of broiler breeds, and to this end it is important that the commercial utility White Wyandotte is maintained.

## Maran

The Maran, which is still seriously sought after today by small breeders and hobbyist egg producers, is noted for its dark brown egg. At best it produces around 200 eggs per year, that is about 100 eggs less than its commercial rivals, and it also has a voracious appetite. Trying to improve its dismal egg production by breeding resulted in poorer shell colour, defeating the whole purpose of keeping the Maran. It is said to originate from the Carnac area of southern Brittany. The French version has lightly feathered legs, while the British breed is clean legged.

*Maran pullet.*

## Welsummer

The Welsummer, from Holland, lays an equally brown egg with a matt shell rather than the glossy shell of the Maran. It is also a poor layer, but with a medium-sized body consumes less feed.

## Barnevelder

The Barnevelder also originates from Holland and is a larger-bodied bird, laying an excellent brown egg in small numbers. None of these three breeds ever became popular with commercial egg producers, but were confined to enthusiasts of the show bench.

## Indian Game

The Indian Game (Cornish Game) originated in Cornwall before the Romans landed and is rumoured to have been

*A trio of Welsummers.*

brought in by the Phoenicians. Although they are extremely poor egg producers, their very broad compact breast with high meat to bone ratio was appreciated by early geneticists, who were responsible for breeding the original broiler table birds.

## Old English Game

This is smaller than the Indian Game, but nevertheless was often used for crossing for table purposes.

## Leghorn

The Leghorn is the most commonly known light breed today. It originated from the Port of Leghorn in Italy and was shipped by sea captains to American ports to be sold to local traders. They arrived in many colours and even at that time

quickly established themselves as very prolific white-egg layers. One batch arriving just a few years later were White, one cockerel and several hens. These were purchased by a wealthy fruit and vegetable trader who took them home to his wife in the countryside. Both became smitten with these white birds, selling off their collection of Brown, Black, Cuckoo and Yellow Leghorns to concentrate on the White.

During the 1870s the first Whites were imported into Britain and Brown Leghorns followed a year or so later. The British breeders, attracted by this prolific egg producer, improved it still further. It was soon realized that by crossing the Leghorn hen with the Rhode Island Red male a very hardy, prolific crossbreed was achieved, with a lower appetite than the heavy breeds which made it even more viable. These crosses remained popular

*Large White Leghorn hen.*

up to the late 1960s, at which time the public demanded and were prepared to pay more for brown eggs, causing the eventual demise of these white-egg producing birds in Britain.

It is interesting to note that during its heyday the three main breeds used when crossing were the Rhode Island × Black Leghorn (in demand by those living in the north of England), the Rhode × Brown Leghorn in the Midlands and the Rhode × White Leghorn in southern England. It is not clear how this division came about, but the Rhode × White Leghorn was the last to disappear from commercial laying units in Britain, although the White Leghorn hybrid is still in demand in hotter climates throughout the world.

Light breeds are notorious for being 'non sitters'.

## Ancona

The Ancona, apart from its colour, is very

similar to the Leghorn. It was an excellent layer of white eggs as the bird matured early and, being a true light breed, had a small appetite. The disadvantage at the time was that it was extremely nervous and flighty, likely to hit the roof should someone venture near the pen without warning. These days it is only sought after as a very attractive show bird.

## Minorca

This was once one of the most popular breeds in this country, but unfortunately its high utility qualities were destroyed by exhibition breeders who bred for exaggerated show points; this, combined with the emergence of the Leghorn, resulted in its decline. There is little doubt that in earlier times the Minorca was out-crossed to improve other breeds, especially the Leghorn.

## Legbar

The Legbar was developed between the two world wars as an autosexing breed. The sexing at day old is clearly seen with

*Buff Orpington cockerel.*

*A Cream Legbar in the foreground and Welsummer in the background.*

clear barring on the head and back of the female chick, while the cockerels' barring is ill defined. It is a slightly flighty bird, a characteristic that is due due to the main influence of the Leghorn. The Legbar was produced by crossing the Brown Leghorn with the Barred Rock.

Other breeds included in this category are the Cambar from the Campine, the Dorbar (Dorking), Buff Bar (Buff Orpington), Brockbar (Buff Rock), Brussbar (Brown Sussex) and the Cream Legbar (Araucana), the latter producing lovely blue eggs. There is only one main breeder of these birds left in Britain and probably only two others left in the world so they would be a wonderful challenge for any up and coming breeder to take on.

## Autosexing Breeds

Autosexing breeds – accepted by the Poultry Club of Great Britain for exhibition in 1945 – enable the small enthusiastic breeder to discard cockerel chicks at the time of hatching. This saves them the costly problem of having to grow all chicks until they are old enough to determine the sexes safely (usually at four to six weeks of age), and then of killing off all the cockerels, which account for around 60 per cent of the hatch.

# 2　Housing

Poultry housing is the 'dead stock' of a poultry unit and as such represents a considerable portion of the capital outlay, particularly if the unit is to be run on intensive-type conditions. Much thought should be given to the selection of poultry houses and to their construction because initial mistakes are easily made and costly to rectify.

In estimating the cost of home-made houses compared with those supplied by manufacturers, the saving is frequently more apparent than real. The producer may disregard the value of his own labour, and may also ignore the fact that while building houses he could be more gainfully employed in attending to other work on or away from the holding, and of course the home-made version may not be as well designed and constructed as the factory-built version.

Cheap and inefficient housing, while being a temptation, may prove the more costly investment in the long run, and equally be responsible for the failure of the business. This may be regarded as an exaggeration of the importance of the subject – but it is not. Good housing is essential to the success of any poultry enterprise, for the best stock in the world will fail to give profitable and satisfactory results without it.

As in other phases of poultry farming, moderation should be practised. Over-elaboration is as unnecessary as it is uneconomic. As a general rule, it is wise to avoid houses that have new features, even if manufacturers claim great advantages. More often than not they prove merely to be good selling points. The beginner is well advised to choose designs that have stood the test of time, and from a firm of high repute.

Poultry houses should be built to provide shelter for birds and to ensure comfort and health. They should be labour saving, i.e. doors large and fully opening, etc. These requirements are easily fulfilled, provided it is recognized that the birds are creatures of the open air, and are well protected by nature. The house should give shelter from the wind and rain and provide adequate floor space, perching and nesting accommodation for its inmates. It should be so constructed that extreme changes of temperature over short periods are avoided. The layout and equipment of the house should keep labour costs to a minimum.

There are four basic systems of poultry keeping, excluding battery cages:

1　Free range
2　Fold units
3　Semi-intensive – birds on range yet within fenced pens
4　Intensive – birds kept in deep-litter houses

Each of these systems has been well proven by poultry farmers and small-holders over the last eighty to ninety years. Under informed management each system will enable the laying hen to produce to its potential, and the system chosen will depend entirely on soil type, available location and, in some cases, its suitability to fit in with the owner's other occupation. More than one system may be adopted depending on prevalent conditions and whether the producer intends to rear his own pullets as well as produce eggs.

## FREE RANGE

The first and foremost condition of the genuine free-range producer is that he has sufficient ground to work with. On medium loam, stocking densities should be no more than 247 birds per hectare (100 birds per acre). With very heavy clay or sandy soil, however, it may be necessary to reduce the numbers slightly. To increase the stocking density on a given area of land without a rest between batches will increase the incidence of disease, especially in respect of parasitical worms.

Poultrymen sometimes speak of keeping birds free range at a stocking density of 1,000 birds per hectare (400 per acre); this is not a reasonable or practical interpretation of genuine free range. It is only possible to work on the basis of a maximum of 375 birds per hectare (150 per acre) if the house or houses are moved to another site away from existing stock at the end of each laying season. For those only wishing to keep 6 or 12 birds, then an area of 5 sq. metres (6 sq. yards) per bird is sufficient. Birds can then be alternated between runs, the frequency depending on local soil conditions, time of year and weather, so preventing either run from becoming fowl sick.

*Two free-range poultry field houses housing new pullets.*

*A small portable poultry ark.*

## Protection

When setting up a free-range unit, that is one without individual runs, often little thought is given to protective fencing, which is so necessary to keep out predators, especially during the daytime. The least expensive way is to install electric fencing, of which there are two basic systems on offer. Firstly, for a permanent boundary fence, one or two manufacturers supply hard Australian wooden posts drilled at the appropriate heights to thread a thin hawser wire through, seven strands in all, which is connected to either a battery energizer or an energizer connected directly to a mains supply. It has been proved that foxes do not jump over the top.

Secondly, in recent years electric netting has become very popular; its main drawback is that it is basically designed for mobile runs rather than an *in situ* boundary fence. Only the horizontal lines are electrified, apart from the base line which contains no wire at all. A problem may occur when the fence is left off or the current is broken by a foreign body in some form or other lying across the line(s) and shorting the circuit. When either of these two things happen, the fencing becomes vulnerable to rabbits chewing the lower lines, destroying the tension and at the same time breaking the circuit, giving free entry to rabbits and predators alike. In some cases, foxes jump over it, as the top is clearly defined by its colour.

Electric netting is composed of woven plastic string interwoven with fine wire, which becomes brittle and breaks after a time, shorting the whole of the netting, again allowing rabbits to chew through the base to give free entry to predators. All electric fencing will need grass and weeds trimming regularly, but netting is more quickly affected by short blades of grass and weed than all-metal strands, the latter tending to burn offending projections, so maintaining a steady electrical current.

## Land Use

Over stocking can be successful for a very limited period. Then serious drops in egg production accompanied by high mortality (caused by the land becoming fowl sick), and accompanied by a heavy build-up of parasitical worms, turn free-range egg production into a loss-making exercise, rather than the expected profitable enterprise which the owner can attain under good management.

If the land is available, rotation of the house or houses on fresh, rested sites should be considered. In this way, the fertility of the land is substantially improved and, at the same time, the general health of the birds is maintained by more natural means. It has to be remembered that if, during their period of lay, hens become infected with worms, treatment will have to be administered over a seven-day period, and a further seven days is demanded before eggs from these birds are allowed to be sold for human consumption. Even in the small-

est area, alternative runs, or the movement of the poultry house from one paddock to another, will have a great effect on keeping birds fit and healthy.

## House Design

Small poultry houses with capacities ranging from six to thirty birds are ideal for the small producer. They should be designed to give maximum protection to the bird, winter and summer alike. The framework should be constructed of 4 × 4cm (1½ × 1½in), clad with 1.5cm (½in) shiplap. Both the floor and roof should be clad with 2.5cm, (1in) tongue and grooved boarding, the roof being overlaid with heavy duty mineral felt.

A wooden house so built provides sufficient insulation for both winter and summer, provided that the poultry house is low to the ground. The coolness of the ground helps to keep the house cool in the summer while in the winter the area covered is warmer than exposed land, assisting in maintaining a warmer house. A poultry house built high up off the ground will not be beneficial to the bird, as there is no protection from cold or hot air flows and provides no control of temperature to the house or birds. The roof is where most heat is lost, and a wooden roof overlaid with mineral felt will, to some extent, assist in maintaining temperatures, acting as a partial insulator. If, instead of wood, a corrugated roof is used, it must be insulated beneath to protect birds from extreme heat or cold and draughts. Ventilation inlets should be placed at the front of the house, as close to the eaves as possible. Six birds will require a total ventilation inlet area of 30 sq. cm (4½ sq. in). By using a sliding baffle or shutter, this area may be reduced still further during the winter months. When looking at larger houses, all these factors need to be taken into consideration.

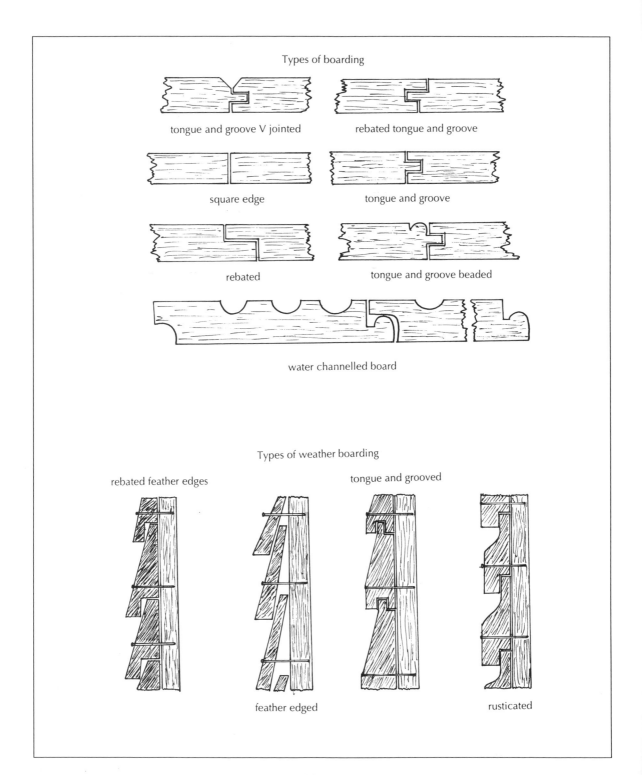

Types of boarding

tongue and groove V jointed

rebated tongue and groove

square edge

tongue and groove

rebated

tongue and groove beaded

water channelled board

Types of weather boarding

rebated feather edges

tongue and grooved

feather edged

rusticated

*Various types of boarding for poultry field houses.*

*A six bird poultry house.*

There are three basic poultry-house designs for free range:

1   Field house. This should be mounted on two substantial skids, 7.5 × 12.5 cm (3 × 5in) to house 50 birds. The house shown has a 2.5 × 2m (8 × 6ft) floor area with four internal perches running the length of the house. Ventilation is at either end of the ridge, with a nestbox at the back of the house. Eggs are collected from the nestbox either by entering the house or from the outside.

The position of the entrance (pophole) at the front of the house, adjacent to the door, has two advantages. Firstly, it faces the front (south), thus avoiding cold winds or rain being driven in to the discomfort of the bird. Secondly, because the hen has to enter at the front, with the nestbox situated at the far end of the house, it is able to clean its feet on the littered floor – so important in wet weather conditions – before entering the nestbox, which reduces significantly the number of dirty eggs. This design of house does not normally have a windowed area.

2   A 200-bird free-range poultry house,

*A Sussex Ark with sliding shutter.*

*A fifty-year-old field house still in use today.*

*A hundred bird poultry house with external nestboxes.*

is the largest poultry house of wooden construction which can be safely moved over reasonably level terrain. This size is popular with producers who have, or anticipate having, total flock sizes of between 1,000 and 2,500 birds. Replacements of 200 birds a time will keep the owner in continuous production of all sizes of all eggs. The use of split flocks avoids excessive bullying, and keeps disease safely under control, ensuring that all birds will range freely. There is no need to fence each flock separately as they will range together quite happily, and can be easily identified by using different-coloured leg rings for each new batch of birds.

3   For those who rely on egg production for part of their total income, and own land that is not suitable to move units around, because it is too hilly or generally uneven, a larger house may be the best and most viable proposition.

If a larger static house is required, the total size of flock individually housed can be as many as 500 before birds are restricted from ranging naturally. Once over this limit, as houses become larger and flock sizes increase in proportion, more and more hens will prefer to stay in their house, due mainly to a higher incidence of territorial peck order. A poultry house with a total capacity of 1,000 laying birds may be split down the middle by a central passageway for feeding and collecting eggs, and may house two separate flocks of 500 birds, one flock being older than the other, provided the house is no wider than 7.5m (24ft).

These larger static houses are normally

*A two hundred bird laying house on skids with fixed polycarbonate windows, baffle eave ventilation and nestboxes installed inside.*

*A two hundred bird free range poultry house. Rollaway nestboxes can just be seen through the windows. Note the baffled inlets just under the eaves and the polycarbonate windows for extra insulation.*

sited on a concrete floor. When the floor is being concreted, place second-hand egg trays below the surface, or mix in the aggregate granulated polystyrene to help insulate the floor. Finish with a smooth render and waterproof sealant. A warm floor will help keep the litter dry and in good condition. Costs may be kept down on the actual building by mounting the house on one or two courses of concrete blocks, reducing the amount of timber used for the sides. Ventilation will be via the side windows, and for the very large house, stale air is taken out through the ridge or ridge cowling.

It is important to remember that the larger the house capacity, the smaller the immediate ground area outside the house is per bird, increasing the density of fouling. This can be overcome by using medium-sized whole flint stone aggregate 6.5cm (2½in). The stone area must be boarded at the edges to prevent hens from spreading the stones too far away from the house.

Alternatively, construct a slatted floor walkway sufficiently strong to take the weight of the operator, and high enough off the ground to provide a reasonable build-up of droppings before cleaning out becomes necessary, every three or four months. Here again, the sides will need to

A slatted walkway on a large free range unit. Note the 'Freedom Foods' large popholes.

Large free range house walkway.

27

be boarded to prevent faeces from spreading out from beneath the slats, especially during very wet weather. With slats there is always a risk of attracting rats, but these can be safely dealt with by pushing small waterproof sachets of poison through the slats.

The siting of the nestboxes is very important. They should be situated in the darkest part of the house, which is usually under the window areas or at the ends of the house.

In general, poultry houses constructed in wood for the genuine free-range bird with a flock capacity of no more than 500 birds will not require further insulation, provided that careful attention to detail

such as design, position and ventilation has been thoroughly and expertly worked out.

Hens must at all times be kept in a well-ventilated (but not draughty), healthy environment where they are able to maintain their natural body temperature without becoming too warm or cold. Over-insulated and under-ventilated houses should be avoided at all costs because they become the perfect breeding ground for disease and are not suitable for birds expected to range both winter and summer. They should also have a large enough area of windows to provide suffi-cient natural daylight within the house for feeding, foraging and dust bathing.

*Birds dust bathing.*

*Dust bathing.*

*Popholes*

These should be positioned either at the front of the house (south) or on the west side. They should under no circumstances face east or north for obvious reasons. The size and number will vary according to the size of the house. Six to 25 bird units will require only one pophole measuring from 30 × 30cm, (12 × 12) to 30 × 45cm, (12 × 18in).

It is not necessarily the number of popholes per house which allow all the birds to come out, but how they are positioned and, at times, what the environment outside has to offer. When 1,000 or more birds are kept as a flock in one house, peck order plays a very important part in preventing the more docile birds from exiting. The more dominant hens – those at the top of the peck order – will stop birds from entering into their territorial space, preventing birds from other areas of the house leaving. Increasing the number or size of popholes per house will in itself have little effect on bird numbers coming out. If too numerous, they may have a detrimental effect on the house's internal environment, especially during the winter when the cold draughts will cause the floor litter to remain damp and wet, encouraging disease and sufficient stress to cause a lowering of egg production.

*Temperature*

Temperatures play a very important part

*Hopper type window where birds have been allowed to rest.*

in production. Internal temperatures of less than −12°C, (10°F) will reduce production by 25 per cent, and no eggs will be laid at −17°C (0°F). At the other end of the scale, temperatures ranging from 10°C to 22°C (50°F to 70°F) are regarded as ideal. When the temperature exceeds 26°C (80°F), particularly with high humidity, birds become distressed and production drops. Light breeds are more able to counteract high temperatures than the heavier breeds. During hot weather a significant drop in temperature during the night will help counterbalance the higher day temperatures. It is true to

say that higher temperatures can be more injurious than the lower temperatures normally experienced in the UK.

*Windbreaks*
Laying hens, as with most other birds, hate driving wind even more than rain, and it is therefore essential that sufficient windbreaks are provided not only around the perimeter but also adjacent to the house. Hedges and shrubs are ideal but are rarely present near larger units.

Straw bales are a cheap alternative and can be placed near the pophole. If bales of straw are placed on the ground in the

30

form of a cross, then no matter which way the wind blows, hens are able to pick the right side and stay out of the house to forage. Two or three bales high will provide a good sheltered area. The length of bales required to run in any one direction needs to be approximately 14m (45ft) per 100 hens.

## FOLD UNITS

Up until the late 1960s fold units were popular for poultry keeping on both small and large areas of ground. They were very suitable for rearing chickens as well as ducks. Housing small important breeding flocks and layers, these units can be a very advantageous part of any poultry enterprise, as:

1   Birds are moved to fresh ground each day;
2   The serious peck order experienced in larger flocks does not exist to the same degree within a small flock, provided the management techniques are strictly observed.

The reason for the fold unit losing much of its popularity in the late 1960s was that it was too labour intensive, and as labour costs soared, so the number of farm employees was drastically reduced. As poultry farming and the breeding of different pure breeds are now once more gaining popularity, so the demand for fold units will continue to increase.

For those with small gardens who spend most of the day away from home at work and wish to keep a few laying birds, safe from marauding dogs and foxes, the

*A very popular Apex type fold.*

fold unit will give around-the-clock protection. It is an extra asset to keen gardeners who like the organic manure birds produce, as well as the valuable assistance they give in killing various garden pests as they scratch and weed each section of the vegetable bed as it becomes vacant, normally during the autumn and winter months. Folds are extremely valuable to fruit trees in gardens and orchards, preventing birds from damaging young fruit trees as they work. The fold is initially cheaper to purchase, and there are several good health factors to be taken into consideration. In the past, it has been found that dairy cows produce more milk off grass where folds have been recently, and that this grass also makes the best quality hay. All birds (apart from ducks) kept in folds should be fed ad lib dry mash and not pellets.

# SEMI-INTENSIVE SYSTEMS

When birds were restricted in fenced runs in the past, the system was called semi-intensive. Nowadays, provided they have an adequate area of ground to live and work on, the eggs from these birds are termed as free range.

## Foxes

Some years ago, as more and more agricultural land was eaten up by property developers and planners, foxes in these areas were left with no alternative but to scavenge from dustbins and other household waste. The fox, with his endearing looks, found instant favour with many town dwellers, and was encouraged to encroach further into towns and cities with bribes of a plentiful supply of dog and cat food. During the breeding season the vixens not only

proliferated with complete litters, but these litters ceased to be controlled by nature, as wild fox litters are (in the wild, about 50 per cent of young die by starvation and other causes).

With the fast expansion of town foxes many residents complained, and so local councils then trapped as many as possible, dumping them in the countryside to fend for themselves. These same foxes are then forced to plunder where they can to survive, and having lost the timidity of their country cousins, create enormous problems for livestock farmers, whether dairy, sheep or poultry. The latter is favourite as it is easier to tackle, and now as a gradual revival is taking place in free-range egg production, its larder is complete. When there is poultry about, rabbits and rats pale into insignificance. For this reason birds need to be securely fenced.

## Constructing the Run

The area required for a semi-intensive run is 5 sq. m, (6 sq. yd) per bird for single pens, and for houses with an alternative run, the area may be halved. The size and height of poultry wire used for penning is 1.8m high × 5cm mesh × 19 gauge (6ft × 2in mesh × 19 gauge). Of this, one third of a metre (1 ft) should be dug into the ground and unless the whole of the top area of the run is securely wired, arms should be attached to the top of each post angled outwards. These arms should measure 1m (3ft) in length. Fix on these brackets 3 strands of barbed wire and tension by hand, so the barbed wire is not too taut. This will prevent a fox from digging under or climbing over.

Semi-intensive runs are not necessarily limited to small flocks and can be constructed to take up to 100 birds. The larger runs were very popular during the time of the village breeder who used them for general cross-breeding, but are now normally used only by small producers in the garden/allotment, orchard or a spare odd-shaped piece of ground.

## Alternative Runs

These enable the producer to rest each run in turn, but where only one run has been constructed it should be rested between batches of birds for at least six weeks. Liberally lime the whole run, paying attention to the fouled area immediately around each house. Water the lime in if it does not rain during the rest period.

# INTENSIVE SYSTEMS (DEEP LITTER)

## House Design

For intensive systems to work effectively the house is the most important part of the enterprise. Houses may be built to house several thousand hens, and they will do well provided pen sizes for each house are no larger than for flocks of 500 birds. Layouts can vary to suit the practical needs of each producer, and provided the floor area and perching space are correct, then the internal layout may be sited to assist all working operations and to enable them to be carried out effectively and efficiently.

The construction of deep-litter houses, as with those for other systems, should be designed to create the best internal environment as is possible, to suit both birds and operator alike. Unless poultry employees are happy working in deep-litter conditions, they will spend as little time in the house as possible, and in doing so, small but important jobs may be missed, resulting in poorer production. All laying birds appreciate companion-ship, this is why the very small flocks will perform better than larger commercial ones in harsher conditions.

The area each bird requires for deep litter is 0.4 sq. m (4 sq. ft). Of this one third will be taken up with perches and two-thirds open floor space. To reduce the floor area will cause an overconcentration of faeces, promoting a build-up of damp infected litter totally unworkable by natural means, and at the same time increasing the amount of ammonia in the house to an unacceptable level and reducing egg production.

## Litter

For litter use either soft dry wood-shavings or wheat straw. The starting layer should be about 10cm (4in) deep, and gradually add as required, building the total depth up to between 23cm and 25cm (9 and 10in). It is very important that the litter should be continually turned and thoroughly mixed to maintain a dry friable texture, so eliminating to a great extent any strong smell of ammonia. Birds can be encouraged to turn the litter themselves by giving them a scratch feed of corn during the afternoon.

## Feed

Hens should have an adlib supply of a good-quality layers mash, fed dry in a sufficient number of waste-free hanging hoppers. Water is ideally arranged over the dropping pits, so that any splash will drop directly into the pit and be kept off the litter.

## Dropping pits

These need not all be sited in the same place but can be sited where it is most beneficial to the house layout. In one house it may be along the wall and in another in the centre. When siting the pit consider how best it can be cleaned out between batches. In many houses there will be large double doors at either end, so that when a central pit is dismantled a tractor and shovel can easily be driven in and through. When the house is not wide or high enough it may be better to site the pit at one end or along the side, whichever is most convenient for easy cleaning out.

Pits should be just under a metre (3ft) high and surrounded by boarding, sheets of corrugated metal, shuttering ply or some other rigid material. Wire sides are not practical because as the droppings build up in the pit the wire is pushed out, and birds are also able to peck at the debris. If the house is fitted with automatic drinkers and one of them floods, only solid sides, provided they are well supported, will stop slurry from seeping out on to the litter. The top of the pit may be constructed of slatted floors or with 7.5cm (3in) mesh where standard perches are placed over the top. Unless the pit is narrow enough for the operator to reach across easily, make sure that it is strong enough for employees to stand on safely.

## Humidity

Large deep-litter houses may be designed without windows, the ventilation relying on baffled air inlets and forced extraction. It is important that the humidity within the house is kept to a minimum without sacrificing temperature in the winter. Once the internal temperature becomes too low then the litter will become cold and damp preventing it from working properly. Much of the success of operating deep litter will depend on how dry and workable it is.

## Nestboxes

These can be either individual or communal. The former is to be preferred because, if well constructed, it gives the hen the quietness and security she needs for laying.

# 3 Ancillary Equipment

Apart from large commercial enterprises, there has been very little innovation of poultry equipment in recent times. In one or two cases supposedly new inventions are the same or very similar to designs of equipment invented during the earlier part of the century.

The real purpose of this chapter is to acquaint the reader with types of equipment available and their correct usage; armed with this information, the producer may then be more confident in making the best selection to suit each unit's own speciality.

## FEEDERS

Feed costs represent up to 75 per cent of the cost of production, yet attempting to restrict wastage by reducing the amount of feed given is false economy, as any restriction may lead to depressed egg production. It is essential to allow birds to be able to feed to their capacity without waste, and this is possible by looking at the alternatives and understanding a few basic principles.

### Space Requirements

When looking at the various designs of feeders, it is important to know the correct feed space each hen needs. For any inline feeder, such as the basic trough, 10cm (4in) of trough space is required per bird. Unless the feeder is against the wall, the measurement includes both sides of the trough, i.e. a trough measuring 61cm (24in) in length will provide 122cm (48in) of space; this is sufficient for twelve laying hens.

When using a circular feeder the birds stand at an angle, not in line, so for this feeder the trough space requirement is 2.5cm (1in) per bird. A circular feeder whose feed base measures 63cm (25in) in diameter is sufficient for 25 birds. It is true that all birds do not feed at the same time and it is always tempting to add more birds without increasing the feeder space. Should this happen, then production is affected and will drop accordingly. Although only a few birds may be seen feeding together they will keep others away rather than let them join in.

It is vital that the figures given are strictly adhered to, and should there be any variance to the rule, then it should be by providing more rather than less space. Some of the more practical producers will add an extra feeder per 100 birds to allow even the lowest of the peck order to have ample chance to feed and produce. The cost of an extra feeder is amply rewarded by the extra eggs produced.

When using troughs, they should be mounted on bricks or shelf brackets, so that they do not become soiled from the continuous scratching of litter. To prevent wastage, do not fill troughs by more than one third, and if some of the older hens are still raking feed out on to the floor, then a 1 × 1in twilweld mesh cut to size can be placed over the top of the feed each time it is replenished.

35

*This kind of feed wastage is not only expensive, it encourages wild birds and vermin.*

*Anti-waste plastic feeding troughs.*

## Circular Feeders

There are two basic types of circular feeder: those made in galvanized metal and those made of hydro plastic. When feeding a dry mash the metal feeders are often very difficult to adjust to allow the feed to fall evenly into the smaller part of the basin. This is because feed tends to vary in coarseness from one batch to another. The flow is also affected by the amount of humidity present at any one time. Once the metal becomes the slightest bit damp, the feed bridges in the overhead cone, and the feeder has to be adjusted accordingly. When the atmosphere dries or if the next bag of mash is coarser, too much invades the feed basin and is subsequently hooked out by busy beaks on to the litter, and is needlessly wasted.

Plastic feeders are not as susceptible to weather or feed changes, the correct feed flow is worked out by the manufacturers, and providing they are suspended at the right height, no waste will occur. It has even been known that where these feeders have been installed, the feed bill has been halved.

Circular feeders are suspended on an adjustable cord and the correct height is to have the base of the feeder 2.5cm (1in) above the bird's back. It may look high, but the average commercial laying hen can feed or drink out of a container whose top lip is 30.5 to 35.5cm (12in to 14in) above the ground. This height is important for another reason: no floor space is lost in the house because birds are able to pass under without hindrance. If feeders or drinkers are left too low to the floor, extra floor area is required to make up for this loss of space.

In all but the system of fold units, space for feeders should be found in the poultry house. At no time should birds be fed the basic feed in outdoor feeders unless these are protected from wild birds and vermin. Both wild birds and vermin will consume

*A treadle-operated automatic feeder.*

*A treadle-operated feeder when not in use.*

*A treadle-operated feeder when in use.*

*A one sided prototype of a Chelwood feeder.*

*Chelwood feeder in use.*

considerable quantities of costly rations, but worst of all, your domestic poultry are subjected to a higher risk of disease. The only feed which may be given on range is if they are given a daily ration of corn. This should be scattered over a large area, preferably on a fresh section of pasture every day.

## DRINKERS

Drinkers will in most cases, except for deep litter, be placed outside the poultry house in the most convenient position for filling, as water is a very heavy item to be carried further than necessary. There are four basic designs to choose from.

*Hens drinking out of water drinker (fount) mounted on a stool.*

## Fount Drinker

The fount drinker, with capacities from 2.25 litres (½ gallon) to 18.25 litres (4 gallons), manufactured in hydro plastic or galvanized steel. Both of these can be used at any stage of the chicken's life, from day old onwards. Galvanized founts should last a lifetime whereas plastic drinkers are inclined to become brittle with age and in general, according to quality, may only last for between 2 to 10 years. Plastic drinkers are easier to clean but are not very practical during freezing temperatures, although they can be emptied each evening. If it freezes during the day they are of little use to any poultry. The space per bird does not appear to be quite so important but a good guide is 1.25cm (½in) per bird for a fount and 2.5cm (1in) per bird for a trough drinker. All drinkers should be raised well off the ground to prevent them from becoming soiled.

## Trough Drinker

The trough drinker has three advantages over the fount:

1   You can always see how much water it contains at any one time.
2   You can see how soiled the water is,
3   In freezing conditions during the day, by floating glycerine on the surface of the water it will only crystallize instead of icing over, enabling the birds to drink freely as and when they

are thirsty. This is very important in maintaining egg production and also frees the operator from continually checking and defrosting drinkers.

The trough is extremely easy to scrub out and can be used for both feed and water. The majority are manufactured in galvanized metal and last for many years, especially if they are kept free from contact with the ground by placing them on bricks or a wooden platform.

## Outdoor Automatic Drinkers

These are made by fitting a ballcock in a tough plastic bowl, usually a cattle-feeding bowl. A galvanized version is also on the market at a slightly higher price.

They are connected to exterior alkathene piping which should be placed below the surface of the ground to protect the pipe from freezing in the winter and from overheating the water during very hot spells. Should the alkathene water pipe become frozen in the winter, the water in the bowls can also be treated with glycerine. These units may be fed directly off a high-pressure water supply, unlike automatic hanging drinkers.

## Low-Pressure Hanging Drinkers

These are supplied directly off a header tank; under no circumstances can they be fed directly from high-pressure mains water. This type of drinker is normally used in deep-litter houses or the very

*Bird drinking out of an auto-ballcock drinker.*

41

large free-range units. The drinker base is adjusted 2.5cm (1in) above the bird's back and suspended over a droppings pits, where inadvertent leaks, or water flicking is enjoyed by all poultry.

A filter is fitted in the drinker assembly to collect algae and any other foreign matter, preventing it from fouling the spring-loaded release washer. If such matter were to pass through to the washer it would prevent it from sealing, thereby causing a continuous leak referred to as an over-flow. Provided any spillage is contained within the area of the pit, little harm is done. However, if left too long without attention then the pressure built up by the extra weight of water may break down the protective side panels and leak slurry over much of the floor area. This will need to be cleaned up to avoid damaging all the remaining dry litter.

If the house is well designed and managed then there is little risk of internal freezing. Should the house freeze, the water in the main adjustment connection barrel immediately above the drinking unit will freeze and break the plastic connector, resulting in a flooded house when the temperature increases.

The circular drinkers are easily cleaned each day by turning and tipping them briskly into a water bucket; drinkers are then automatically refilled with fresh clean water from the header tank. The filter should be checked weekly. Water in the header tank must be kept protected by a cover from dust and insects and so on; there are sanitizers on the market which can be added to kill off algae and harmful bacteria without affecting the birds.

## PERCHES/SLATS

In static poultry houses, field houses and others with solid floors, perches are needed to prevent birds from squatting on the ground on their own droppings; these then heat up to give off unacceptable levels of ammonia.

### Height

The height of the perch is critical because if it is fitted too high off the ground, even if the birds can fly up to it, when jumping down in the morning the sudden landing can upset the reproductive system. Also, if the litter has been allowed to pack down or is too shallow, and because of this presents a hard surface, then a condition known as bumble foot is more likely to occur. The maximum height should be no more than 0.6m (24in). They can be as low as 0.3m (12in) if a very heavy breed is to be housed such as the Buff Orpington. The adjustment will obviously vary according to the height of the house.

### Positioning

Perches are either rested inside wall sockets or built on a removable frame. At no time should they be permanently fixed. They should be fitted in the house to run lengthways and not across. If they run across the width of the house, they obstruct the operator from easy access to nestboxes, cleaning out or picking up birds for collection or handling. Fresh soft nightly droppings will cover the litter over the whole width of the house, making it impossible for laying hens to pass from one end of the house to the other without dirtying their feet and in turn soiling any eggs in the nestbox.

### Construction

Each perch should be made from standard red/yellow deal (softwood), planed smoothly to 4 × 5cm, (1½ × 2in), the top

*Field house showing hinged perch rail in front of the nestboxes.*

this position and, by doing so, their natural feeding time is reduced and egg production is affected. Birds squabbling over perch space can lead to broken bones, especially wing bones.

It is argued in some quarters that the top of the perch should be rough to give birds a better grip. This argument has no sound practical foundation, because within two weeks of birds perching, the top area is roughened by faeces. To avoid an excessive build-up of this they should be scraped off monthly (paint scrapers are ideal for this job).

Deep-litter houses will require the same perch sizes and the same distances between even though they are placed over a droppings pit. In some instances, a slatted floor is preferred to perches.

## Slats

A slatted floor in a well-designed house provides very efficient ventilation helping to maintain good healthy birds. Slats became popular in the late 1930s as they were a cheaper form of flooring for night arks and fold units, and also because by design they distributed poultry droppings evenly over the ground. Houses fitted with slats did not have to be cleaned out nearly as often as solid-floor houses and saved labour. The floor area needs to be checked and scraped monthly to prevent the droppings from clogging up between the slats. Vulnerable areas are mainly in corners or around the edges.

A few well-known breeders incorporated slats in all their poultry houses, including breeding pens. The late Mr Watanabe, a nationally respected breeder of Rhode Island Reds and Light Sussex, was responsible for introducing the slatted-floor system to the UK. Slats are made from the same wood as are used for perches and are cut to 2.5 × 2.5cm (1 × 1in) in size and placed 2.5cm apart, these

edge bevelled either side and fitted at 25.5cm (10in) centres, supported every 1.8m (6ft). Neither sawn or hardwood timber should be used. Sawn wood is very difficult to scrape clean and may cause feet splinters; it is also an ideal hiding place for parasites such as red mite. The use of hardwood prevents birds from gripping securely with their claws and therefore they do not settle as quickly or as well. All perches should be fitted at the same level, or birds will crowd on the highest perch.

When apex-shaped perches are used it can be seen by careful observation that those birds wishing to perch at the highest level will come in earlier to obtain

*Small free range poultry house with a slatted floor positioned over droppings boards.*

being fitted to a frame strong enough to take the weight of the operator.

If slats are to be used as a floor in a static free-range house then by raising the droppings pit by approximately 0.75m (2ft 6in) off the ground, there will be a sufficient cubic capacity to contain 12 months of droppings without cleaning out. The floor area required for birds on slats is normally half of that required in a solid-floor house, and is 58 sq. cm (9 sq. in) per bird.

## NESTBOXES

There are two basic types of nestbox: the individual and the communal.

## Individual

Individual nestboxes usually measure 30 × 30 × 30cm (12 × 12 × 12in). These may be fitted in a row on one level or several rows tiered above each other. Where this style of nestbox is fitted along one side of the house it may be designed as a roll-away. A roll-away nestbox has a slanted base, which encourages eggs to roll to a main catchment area to prevent the hen from damaging her own or other eggs; it also prevents the egg from becoming dirty from the bird's feet. This also prevents egg eating, as birds are unable to reach the eggs once laid.

In the summer, the egg is cooled more quickly than those being continually sat on. The main disadvantage of rows of

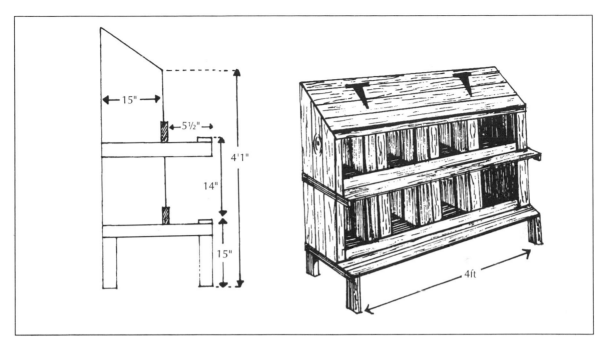

*Nestboxes.*

*Roll-away nestboxes in a two hundred bird free range house.*

nestboxes is that hens have a favourite box and some would rather pile on top of each other, thus suffocating the lower birds, rather than sitting in an empty box further along the row. This behaviour encourages some birds to lay on the floor.

## Communal

Communal nestboxes can also be designed as roll-away, and with the frontage covered, except for the entrance hole, give the hen a dark quiet area to settle and lay. The smaller 6-bird house will require only one box 30 deep × 60 long × 30cm high (12 × 24 × 12in). If birds try to crowd at one end, without a solid partition, they are able to spread out.

## Positioning

Nestboxes should be placed in the darkest corner of the house, which is invariably directly below the windows, and should be

*Communal nestbox with wire base for six birds.*

*Home made nestboxes fitted below a window. Note the perch sockets.*

sited lower than the perches, so that birds are not encouraged to perch in them. An alighting perch should run along the front of the nestbox for birds to alight on. This, if hinged, when folded up will prevent young pullets from perching in the nest-boxes at night. Keep nestboxes closed for about two weeks after birds are housed to enable them to establish their night-time roosting position on the perches or slats.

One individual nestbox is required for every four to five birds, depending on whether they are light or heavy breeds (most hybrids are included in the medium breed bracket). A communal nestbox with a floor area of 5,574 sq. cm (864 sq. in) or 46cm deep × 122cm long (18in deep × 48in long) is sufficient for 50 laying hens. These may be tiered to produce a 100-bird communal laying nestbox.

## Flooring

Make the floor of 1.25 × 1.25cm, (½ × ½in) heavy-duty wire mesh or weldmesh, and cover with a light layer of straw. The advantage of this type of floor is that the nestbox remains fresh and the litter dry, keeping eggs cleaner. If birds do try to crowd on top of one another, then those at the bottom are still able to breathe. It also acts as an anti-broody device.

# 4   Breeding

Throughout the years the poultry breeder has endeavoured to improve his breeding stock, enjoying some measure of satisfaction as his breed strains gradually improve. This achievement is attained only by strict selection of parent stock, using all the records kept at his disposal and drawing on his own practical knowledge to make the final decision. Only the very large breeders, most of whom are centred in America, can afford the high costs of selection by laboratory techniques, and even they get it wrong now and again as they try to push their goals beyond the realm of practical reality. The small breeder, in most cases, has to rely completely on his own knowledge and skill.

It would be easy if selection could be based on one character alone, but unfortunately this is not the case. The most important factors to be considered are: vigour, disease resistance, hatchability, rearability, quick feathering, egg production, egg size, shell texture and colour, body size and shape, colour and depth of plumage and so on. The latter may not be deemed so important to intensive egg producers, but with free-range egg production on the increase, today's breeders will once again be looking at this important trait. The breeding or retaining of vigour is more important than any other characteristic, as without this, all other breeding requirements become insignificant.

At one time, many breeders thought that good breeding skills were just a matter of selecting the best cockerels, and that by putting them together with the best hens, there was an equal mixing of blood lines. Nothing could be further from the truth. To avoid becoming too complicated, there are specialist breeding books dealing more extensively with this subject. This chapter involves basic information which the reader will need to know and understand before he embarks on any poultry breeding exercise.

## MATING

Cockerels should not be introduced until pullets are at least 18 weeks of age and young males at least 24 weeks of age. In the act of mating, the semen in the reproductive cells of the cockerel is ejaculated into the cloaca of the hen and travels up through the öviduct to unite with the egg yolk (ovum) shortly after it leaves the ovary. Enough semen swims up to fertilize between 12 and 14 eggs at one mating; this enables a young vigorous cockerel to cover successfully as many as 80 hens in a flock, although I do not advocate this as standard procedure.

For outdoor breeding, good fertilization is achieved with one cockerel per 25 birds. If 100 breeding hens are running together as one flock, it is advisable to put in 5 or 6 cockerels, preferably those which have been reared together. It is not practical to add any further cockerels at a later date should any loss be incurred, as these would be attacked and probably killed. By starting with one or two extra cockerels in the pen, the breeder is able to run successfully through the breeding season even if one or two cockerels die or lose condition. Cockerels can always be taken out but never added.

On observation, unless there are many hidden areas for all cockerels to work without interference from each other, then the one at the top of the peck order will do the majority of the work, with the second in line covering the remainder of the birds. Should too many cockerels be put in a pen of birds, they will spend most of their time pushing one another off each time one tries to mount, and fertility will be adversely affected. Where birds are paired, one male to one female, fertility is often very poor. It is much better to pen one male to six females or more, for good incubation results.

Cockerels being reared together as stock cockerels will from about fourteen weeks of age begin to assert their sexual authority, resulting in the one at the bottom of the peck order being habitually raped. If this bird is taken away, then the next will be trodden and so on. To alleviate the problem, some breeders will put in an older male, one of the previous year's birds as this sometimes helps in keeping the younger birds under control. The other method is to run two or three of the older hens not required for breeding with them. It not only prevents the cockerels from attacking one another, but gives them necessary experience before they are introduced to the breeding pen.

Finally, when a pen is made up of one male to several females, it is sometimes found that one or two hens are not fertile. This may be because they are not compatible with this particular cockerel. Where more than one cockerel is used in a pen, providing pen numbers are sufficient, this problem is reduced, if not resolved. The other alternative is to separate infertile hens, placing them in another pen with a different male, who may be found to be compatible.

## SELECTION

There are two types of chromosome: sex chromosomes and ordinary chromosomes (autosomes). The latter are responsible for all the characteristics of the offspring, and since the number of characteristics far exceeds the number of chromosomes, each chromosome contains a number of genes, which apart from determining the sex, are responsible for egg production, shell colour, egg weight, body size and so on.

When the ovum is fertilized, there is a rearrangement and recombination of the various factors carried by both the male and female birds, and it is how this rearrangement is carried out which produces the inherited characteristics of both male and female.

This may seem a somewhat haphazard method to the reader, but it is not entirely so. There are cockerels which when crossed with certain females produce what the breeder is looking for; other cockerels will produce the reverse, and this is called 'nicking'. Through the use of modern technology the very large hatcheries are able, by a selection of blood samples, to select male and female birds which, when mated, will produce progeny of commercial and economical value. The smaller breeders, though, will have to draw from their own practical knowledge and records to achieve a similar success. It just takes longer.

### Cockerels

In very general terms, the cockerel should be one which has been selected from a dam (his mother) that has produced all the traits which are required to be passed

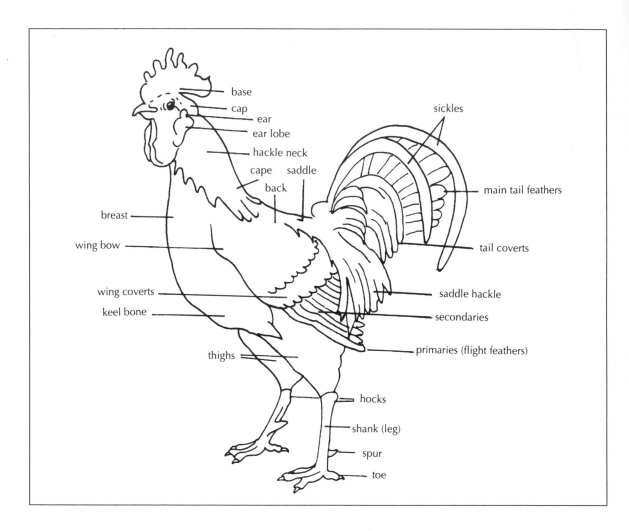

*Parts of the cockerel.*

on to the next generation of chicks. These particular cockerels should be marked at birth by the breeder, and during the growth period be observed and re-selected, so that when the new breeding season arrives, the final selection is taken from those who have lived up to the standard the breeder is aiming for.

The cockerel is the most important part of the breeding pen. The hen, although supporting the cockerel traits, will need to conform to correct body size and shape, which are the main two characteristics she will pass on. This was quickly recog-

nized by breeders many decades ago, who found that by crossing a Rhode Island Red with a Light Sussex, the male progeny took on the body frame of the dam, and the females the egg production and other traits of the sire.

The cockerel must come from good egg-producing stock, and have grown quickly and well with early feather coverage. He must exude vigour and vitality with a slightly aggressive temperament. He should be well muscled and firm to handle; his eye colour should be bold and even, surrounding a perfectly round black pupil. If there are any irregularities in the eye colour, such as a yellow or green ring circling the pupil, or the pupil is oval shape or split then the bird must be rejected, as these eye deformities represent a later health problem. His comb should be correctly serrated, as per the breed requirements, and his wattles even in size. Legs must be clean and strong, toes straight and not curled inwards. Without sound legs and feet, it will be very difficult for him to mount a young breeding hen.

It is very important that during the selection process, the breeder sticks strictly to his preconceived specifications, and if in any particular year the ideal standards have not been achieved by a few or more of the next generation, they must be discarded and the older proven males kept on. This applies also when the selection of females takes place.

If birds have been trap-nested – an expensive business these days – then during the selection of new birds to enter the breeding pens, you must have all the appropriate records available, using them as a back-up to birds which take your eye, and not as a means to an end. Young birds from trap-nested stock, that have been wingbanded or marked by toe-punching at day old and their number or mark added to their parents' records, provide the breeder with access to each young bird's parental egg records. This knowledge of each grower's pedigree is invaluable to the selection of new birds. However, if no trap-nesting has been carried out, all is not lost, it just requires more experience and patience to upgrade the flock each year, and it is basically the flock records that have to be relied on.

## Eggs

Another very important part of selection is at the egg stage; here, eggs are selected on shell quality, size (weight), shape and shell colour. No sub-standard eggs should be considered for incubation. Flock records of the parent stock are very important, as these will show all facets of their production. Hens that are not up to standard must be culled (taken out from the flock) as soon as possible, and ailing birds cannot be bred from. This was one of the reasons why, years ago, poultry breeders would select future breeding stock only from birds in their second season of lay, as in this way any weakness in the strain had already manifested itself. Set eggs from your own replacements when they have been laying for 16 to 18 weeks, and only from eggs which have reached the required standard, the minimum of which is 60 grams. Obviously, this will vary a little according to the breed, but if you require birds to produce a large number of large-size eggs, then this basic weight should be adhered to, gradually increasing as birds mature. Once hens in the second season of lay have nearly reached full production, as egg size will already be large, eggs may be set. If eggs from first-year pullets are to be used for the selection of the following year's breeding stock, then the further they are into lay, the better chance the breeder will have of assessing accurately which eggs are to be incubated. If chicks hatched from eggs set too early are destined to be kept as future breeders, the owner may throw away years of hard work.

## Females

Females for future breeding should be selected on a very strict basis. In the long run it is cheaper to cull out, if in doubt, than to try to maintain flock numbers because of demand for a particular breed. All birds should be handled individually, noting the body size and shape. A body with plenty of depth is an important

# EGG ASSESSMENT CHART

**C. R. SHAW**
MORVILLE HEATH
BRIDGNORTH
SHROPSHIRE, WV16 5NA
TEL.: (074631) 210
FAX.: (074631) 411

BREED.............. THIS ASSESSMENT PERIOD..............

PEN.............. TOTAL ASSESSMENT PERIOD..............

| IDENTIFICATION | GRADING | | | | | | | | SHELL | | | | TRAP NEST RECORD | | | | % EGGS SET | REMARKS |
|---|---|---|---|---|---|---|---|---|---|---|---|---|---|---|---|---|---|---|
| | | | | | | | | | | | | | This Assessment Period | | Total Assessment Period | | | |
| RING / WB | 1 | 2 | 3/1 | 3/2 | 4 | 5 | 6 | R | Brown | Tinted | White | Quality | Egg Nos. | % Production | Egg Nos. | % Production | | |
| | | | | | | | | | | | | | | | | | | |
| | | | | | | | | | | | | | | | | | | |
| | | | | | | | | | | | | | | | | | | |
| | | | | | | | | | | | | | | | | | | |
| | | | | | | | | | | | | | | | | | | |
| | | | | | | | | | | | | | | | | | | |
| | | | | | | | | | | | | | | | | | | |
| | | | | | | | | | | | | | | | | | | |
| | | | | | | | | | | | | | | | | | | |
| | | | | | | | | | | | | | | | | | | |
| | | | | | | | | | | | | | | | | | | |
| | | | | | | | | | | | | | | | | | | |
| | | | | | | | | | | | | | | | | | | |
| | | | | | | | | | | | | | | | | | | |
| | | | | | | | | | | | | | | | | | | |

*Measuring the abdomen of a bird in full lay (a three finger span between pelvic bones.*

*Measuring the abdomen of a bird in laying condition four fingers between pelvic bones and end of the breast bone.)*

pointer to a potential good layer; the handler should be able to place four fingers between the pelvic bones and the rear of the breast bone. There is a certain feel to well-grown birds which is impossible to explain on paper. When handled, they just feel good, solid yet not fat, well and evenly muscled.

A potential stockman will quickly learn to recognize the 'feel' if they spend some time with an experienced breeder, learning to handle not only 18-week-old

pullets but birds of varying ages. If handed a varied selection of birds in the dark, it should be possible for experienced handlers to select those which conform to the required standards. There is no alternative to experience and sound practical training which comes from the practice of handling a great number of birds over the years, and nothing can replace it.

With pure-breed mating it is rare, but possible, to get a sudden reversion of birds

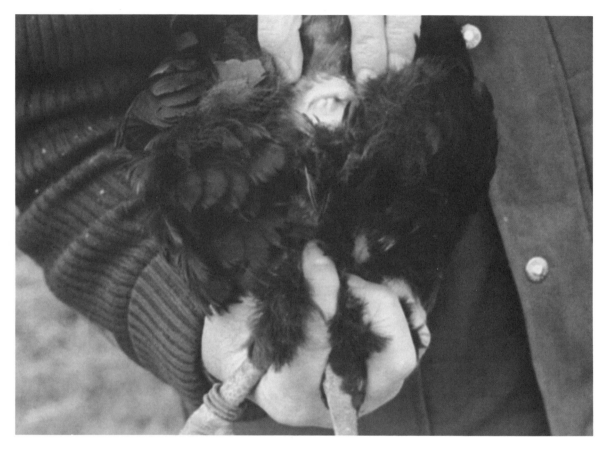

*The vent of a layer is large, moist and cresent shaped.*

relating to their ancestors, but this must not be regarded as proof of some impurity of the parent stock.

There is an ever-increasing demand for crosses other than today's commonly available hybrids, and because of this the smaller breeders are selecting once again popular crosses of bygone years to supply a rejuvenated market. Because of the cost of vent sexing for the smaller producer, the breeder will look to crosses which, on hatching, demonstrate their sex by various differentials in colouring and marking.

## SEX LINKAGE

Where genes are situated on autosomes it makes no difference in the progeny whether a dominant gene of a given pair comes from the sire or dam. However, in the case of genes born of sex chromosomes it makes a great deal of difference.

If a Light Sussex cockerel is mated to a Rhode Island female, the silver gene is crossed with the gold gene and the silver gene being dominant, all the progeny will take after the male and look like Sussex. When this is reversed and the Rhode Male is crossed with the Sussex female, the true sex linkage is seen and the female chicks will be brown taking after the sire, while the male chicks take after the dam and are Light Sussex in appearance. At day old the pullet chicks are brown and the cockerel chicks are white. The reason for the popularity of the cross was that it greatly improved egg production for the commercial industry. The cockerels were also kept for table when caponization was legal, although few were killed before 18 to 24 weeks of age. This is now not viable with the cost of feed.

Other popular crosses at one time are again attracting interest from a new generation of the more serious hobbyists, and are described below.

## Brown Leghorn × White Wyandotte

A useful dual-purpose cross for table and egg production. The shell colour is cream, which becomes mottled very quickly giving the appearance of being stale only a few days after being laid. Because of an infusion years ago of Leghorn by some breeders wishing to improve egg production, the sexing of this cross is only really successful if the White Wyandotte Line has maintained its true 'silver factor', in which case most of the pullet chicks are buff brown with gold stripes running down the back. The cockerel chicks are yellowish cream, though some may be greyish or greyish-black; those completely black are invariably pullets.

## Rhode Island Red × White Wyandotte

This was an extremely popular dual-purpose cross at one time but because of difficulties experienced in accurate sexing it lost some of its popularity. Sexing recognition is similar to that of the Brown Leghorn × Wyandotte; the pullet chicks are normally much redder and darker as is to be expected from a Rhode sire.

## The Brown, White and Black Leghorn Crosses

The Leghorns are the males. These were used extensively throughout the UK at one time because of the fact that these crosses produced a lighter pullet with a lower feed conversion, which was a very important economic factor to the commercial egg producer. The demise of this cross was due to the public preferring a brown-coloured egg shell. The White Leghorn hybrid is still extremely popular in countries which prefer white-shelled eggs or have no choice.

## Indian Game × Light Sussex

This was bred for table purposes only; it produces the finest-tasting carcass with excellent conformation, but unfortunately Indian Game of any quality are difficult to procure these days. When hatched, they produce the same coloration differences as the Rhode × Sussex.

## Sex Linkage by Barring

The Rhode Island Red × Plymouth Barred Rock is marketed as a Hybrid and is an extremely popular bird for genuine free-range units, maintaining the older characteristics of size, vigour, disease resistance and depth of feather. This cross is called, 'Sex Linkage by Barring'. The pullet chicks are black except for the underneath parts, and the cockerel chicks are black with a white spot on top of the head. Other breeds used for sex linkage by barring are Rhode Island Reds, Black Leghorns and other gold line males. When mated with barred females, such as the Cuckoo Maran, North Holland Blue and Scots Grey, all the pullets when mature are basically black and the cockerels barred.

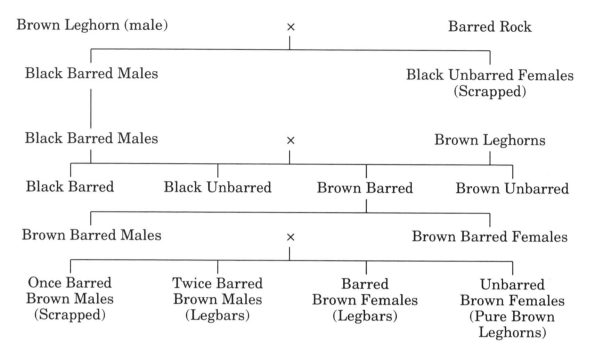

Diagram showing make-up of the legbar.

## Autosexing

The principle of sex linkage has been used when evolving the autosexing breeds, but sex distinction by the down colour of chicks at birth has been applied within one breed.

The first of these was produced in 1929 at Cambridge by Professor R.C. Punnett and Mr M.S. Pease, as a result of experiments in crossing the Golden Campine with Barred Plymouth Rocks. The Barred Plymouth Rocks, North Holland Blue, Cuckoo Leghorn and Maran are all basically black chicks. The autosexing breeds are pure breeds which when bred pure will produce chicks which can be easily sexed at hatching. It is possible to sex their chicks as the pullets have distinct striping down the back, whereas the cockerels' striping is indistinct and 'washed out'.

The example given above is the classic way to make the autosexing breeds, but results in too high a wastage for small-scale breeders. The origins of these new breeds are indicated by the names:

*Cambar – Campine
Gold Legbar – Brown Leghorn
*Dorbar – Silver Grey Dorking
*Buffbar – Buff Orpington
Rhodebar – Rhode Island Red
*Brockbar – Buff Rock
*Brussbar – Brown Sussex
Welbar – Welsummer
Cream Legbar – Araucana

*Indicates those breeds which no longer exist.

This list is a challenge to young interested breeders everywhere who wish to perpetuate these lines. It is important to note that when first selecting the cockerels to be used for barring, they themselves must be clearly and distinctively marked at hatching.

Breeds may be improved by introducing new blood on the female side; for example: Rhode Legbar males crossed with Rhode Island Red females, the female progeny of which can be mated with Rhodebar males.

If Legbar males are crossed with Rhode Island Red females, most pullets will exhibit willow-coloured legs and the cockerels yellow legs. This also applies to the Legbar × Brown Leghorn. Considerable experience may be required to sex barred breeds. The breeder must select a good strain when carrying out this cross. Male chicks of these breeds are usually lighter in down coloration than the female, and have a well-spread white head spot, with silvery white in head and throat, and the legs and toes a dusky yellow. Female chicks have a smaller head spot, are usually black about the face with white spots, and have dark legs with yellow at the tip of the toes.

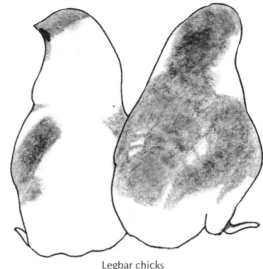

Legbar chicks
The male chick is on the left

Day old Legbars
Three daughters and a son

## VENT SEXING

This is an impossible method of sexing for the lay-person. A long period of expensive practical training is required to become competent and accurate by this method. Such people are trained professional operators, employed mainly by the large commercial broiler hatcheries, for broiler chicks that cannot be feather sexed.

## FEATHER SEXING

This type of sexing is used by one of the

Silver Cambar chicks
The cockerel is in the foreground

57

major broiler breeders who has bred, by careful crossing, chicks that can be accurately sexed by looking at their wing feathers after hatching. It is very simple to learn, but is of little consequence unless the reader has a breed or cross which produces the right characteristics. Sexing is carried out by looking at the wing feathers; in the cockerel the top flights are shorter than the under flights, while the pullet's top flights are longer than the under flights. An experienced sexer is able to sex at the rate of 1,000 chicks per hour with 98 per cent accuracy. I am not aware of any pure breeds that can be feather sexed with the same scale of accuracy.

Feather sexing can be carried out at about 14–15 weeks of age with most breeds. This is done by checking the saddle feathers of each young bird. If the new growing feathers are rounded at the end and relatively dull, the bird will be a pullet. The new emerging saddle feathers of a cockerel are pointed and very shiny. As these feathers grow there is a distinct silky edge to each feather.

## VISUAL SEXING

It is possible to sex visually at between 4 and 5 weeks of age. The operator will see that the young pullet chicks have feathered up almost completely, and have well-developed tail feathers. They will be slightly smaller than the opposite sex, have no noticeable comb or wattles (with maybe the exception of the Leghorn) but are streamlined and sleek in appearance. The young cockerel chick may still have very few body feathers, has thicker legs and leg joints, and a larger head with a small reddening comb and wattles. This is with the exception of light breeds such as the Leghorn, where the males will be fully feathered but showing already a very discernible comb and wattles.

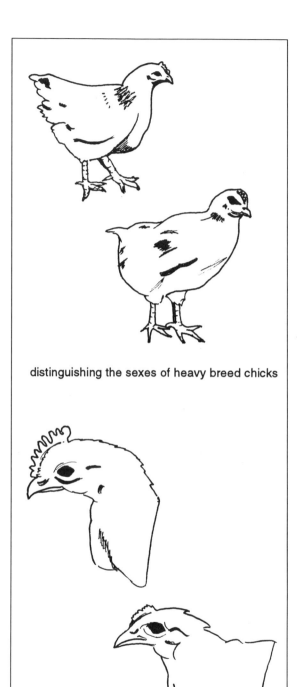

distinguishing the sexes of heavy breed chicks

sexing light-breed chicks

# OUT-BREEDING, IN-BREEDING AND LINE-BREEDING

Out-breeding means the mating of unrelated birds. It can imply the mating together of unrelated birds of the same breed or of different breeds. It is popular because the resultant progeny develop greater vigour, called hybrid vigour, and there is no requirement to cross breeds to obtain this vigour, but simply to cross unrelated blood lines. It gives the breeder an opportunity to introduce into the flock desirable genes.

On the down side, there is an equal risk of introducing undesirable factors. Out-breeding always tends to produce a heterogeneous flock which will not breed true, and the individuals in the flock may be dissimilar. It is basically popular for the crossing of two different breeds, and it should be understood that the parentage from either side must come from good-quality stock.

In-breeding or line-breeding is required for fixing all desirable factors within the flock, producing a homogeneous flock which is identical. The disadvantage of this type of breeding, unless it is very expertly carried out, is that the evils of degeneracy will merge with birds lacking vigour. This is experienced by several breeders of show poultry who, once they have produced a few winning birds, are afraid to incorporate new blood lines for fear of losing what they have. The unfortunate result is poor fertility, hatching and rearing, plus deformity in some of the few chicks which actually hatch.

# A VICIOUS COCKEREL

Some breeds are more aggressive than others, and from time to time a breeder will experience a cockerel that will attack anyone entering the pen. The simple answer is to replace it with another bird of equal quality, but this is not always possible.

When you enter the pen and the cockerel charges at your legs, pick him up, holding him securely resting on your arm, and stroke and generally make a fuss of him. After a few minutes put him down in the pen. It may take only one such session to cure him, but if not, repeat the action until he treats you with utmost respect. To carry a stick and dustbin lid every time you enter the pen is self-defeating, and will probably cause him to become even more aggressive.

# 5 The Reproductive System

## FORMATION OF THE EGG

One has to think first of an egg as a living embryo which nature has provided with adequate protection so that, if fertilized and incubated, it will produce after three weeks (according to the breed) a healthy young chick.

Pullet chicks when hatched are born with very large numbers of undeveloped ova in the ovary, the ovary being located high up in the abdominal cavity. The number of ova which eventually develop into yolks (ovums) will depend on two basic facts: its genetic breeding, and how well each bird has been reared.

The ova grow very slowly until their diameter is 6mm. As each pullet reaches sexual maturity the rate of growth of the ovum (yolk) is enormously increased at the rate of 6mm per day. The fully formed yolk takes seven days to develop from 6mm to full ripeness.

It is the blood which supplies dissolved proteins and fatty acids to feed the developing ova. If an egg is hard boiled and then cut in half, it can be seen that the yolk is made up of concentric layers of dark and light colours. First, a pear-shaped structure of light yolk is formed below the germinal disc; this is then covered during the day (hours of light) by a layer of dark yolk and then light yolk during the night. The yolk is held in a fine membrane called the follicle, which is attached by a thick stalk to the ovary.

When fully ripe, the follicle splits along the line of the stigma, releasing the yolk from the ovary. It is then recognizable as a yolk and is held in shape by a viteline membrane. The ruptured follicle later degenerates.

It is at the time when the yolk is released, and before it has entered the funnel of the oviduct, that the laying bird is most vulnerable. Any sudden panic may cause the yolk to bypass the oviduct and drop down into the body cavity, causing almost certain death.

As the yolk is released, it is drawn towards the oviduct's funnel entrance by the repeated advances and recessions of the rim of the funnel, and on entry it is gradually propelled down the oviduct by a series of peristaltic waves. Once in the magnum, with the help of these circular motions the yolk is wrapped by the thick albumen which forms about half the egg white in total. At the same time, the spiralling action causes two white – and as yet invisible – cords to become attached to either end of the yolk. These are called the chalazae, and are continuous with the outer layer of the yolk membrane; they anchor the yolk to the final egg.

The next stage is at the isthmus, where the shell membranes are deposited in the form of liquid threads which interweave and solidify to form continuous membranes. The outer membrane is thicker than the inner, and they lie together except where the air space appears.

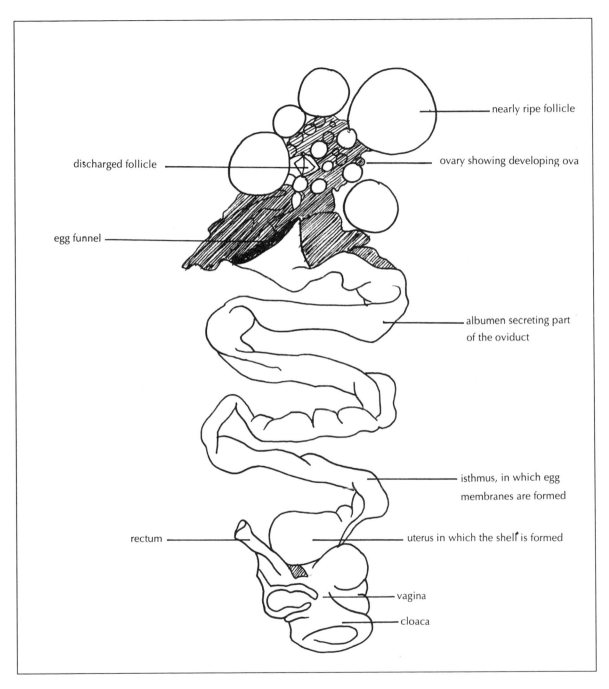

nearly ripe follicle

ovary showing developing ova

discharged follicle

egg funnel

albumen secreting part
of the oviduct

isthmus, in which egg
membranes are formed

rectum

uterus in which the shell is formed

vagina

cloaca

*The female reproductive system.*

The partially formed egg now passes down to the uterus, (shell gland) where the shell is laid down, and it is during this process that the thin albumen is drawn by way of osmosis through the shell, to complete the egg. The last and final stage before the egg is laid takes place in the vagina where the pigmentation is added. After this the cuticle covers the finished product and is the final protective barrier to prevent bacteria from passing through the shell. The cuticle also controls, to a certain extent, the humidity within the egg.

The cuticle is not water soluble, and can only be removed by overwashing at too high a temperature, or by the use of abrasive cleaning materials. Warren and Scott produced the following figures for the length of the different parts of the oviduct of an average light breed hen: infundibulum 3.2cm, isthmus 10.5cm, uterus 10.3cm, and vagina 4.9cm. Ovulation takes place within 14–75 minutes after the previous egg has been laid, and the times taken for the yolk to pass through the different parts of the oviduct as it gradually forms into a complete egg are: infundibulum 18 minutes, magnum 174 minutes, isthmus 74 minutes, uterus and vagina 20 hours 40 minutes. Just over 25 hours are taken between ovulation and the laying of an egg.

If the average time between ovulation and the laying of the previous egg is taken as 30 minutes, the intervals between the laying of successive eggs in the same clutch is rather more than 25½ hours. The experienced producer will already appreciate the fact that each bird lays at a slightly later time than the previous day, and that some good layers will lay up to and over 7–14 days without rest. The best layers lay in the region of 345 eggs in 365 days, which is only two extra eggs more than the 25½-hour clock provides for.

During the period of lay, birds must be treated with the utmost consideration in respect of peace and quiet, and if any have to be handled for one reason or another, they should be handled correctly and firmly, causing as little stress as possible, to them or any others of the flock which may be nearby. Layers kept in large multiflock units experience a higher mortality from reproductive disorders than those kept in small flocks or battery cages. Birds in breeding pens are also more susceptible to a slightly higher incidence of egg peritonitus (**see** chapter on Diseases), even though cockerels will by and large mate when the hen comes off the nest or very soon after.

The shape of an egg is determined by the diameter of the isthmus and uterus, the quantity of albumen secreted, and the muscular activity exerted by the walls of the uterus. The peristaltic waves exert maximum pressure behind the egg and so force it through the sphincter muscle of the vent, blunt end first. The egg is completely rigid when laid and not, as has been suggested from time to time, soft and hardening immediately it is produced.

All the eggs of each bird will be identical, with the exception that they increase in size as the birds become older. Egg size will increase the longer the bird is in lay to her maximum uterus expansion. The length of time it will take for a pullet gradually to increase the size of the eggs she lays will depend on her age when she was brought into lay, her genetic breeding, nutrition and outside temperature.

It is possible with small flocks, by arranging each day's eggs in order, to spot the more productive hens. Once the eggs can be identified with particular birds, an individual record of each bird may be kept without the requirement of trap-nesting. However, this can only be sensibly achieved in very small flocks.

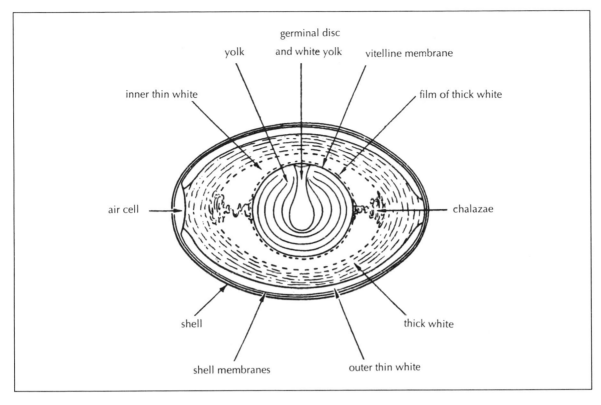

*The composition of an egg.*

## COMPOSITION OF THE EGG

The egg consists of five parts: the germinal disc, the yolk, the albumen or white, the shell membranes and the shell. It is essentially a complex reproductive system designed to provide food and give every possible protection to the ensuing embryo. All five parts form a series of defensive mechanisms, which control harmful bacterial infections from passing through to the centre of the egg, and also contain any inherent disease.

This natural protective system is not perfect, but as near perfect as nature can make it. For example, in the few eggs found to have been infected with either Salmonella Enteritidis or Typhimuium, the natural barriers within the shell

|  | Ash % | Water % | Protein % | Fat % |
|---|---|---|---|---|
| New laid, whole egg | 65.9 | 12.83 | 10.59 | 10.68 |
| Yolk | 48.63 | 17.58 | 32.24 | 1.55 |
| Albumen | 87.00 | 11.00 | 0.20 | 0.80 |

kept the bacteria under control, so that one person would have to eat an enormous quantity of eggs at one sitting to suffer from even the slightest food poisoning. When the egg is broken and exposed to cross-infection from meat and other food products, salmonella is allowed to increase unabated, unless the broken egg or prepared food is kept at the right temperature in a refrigerator. It is interesting to note, that dried-egg products have proved more vulnerable to infection than those made directly from whole egg under good standards of hygiene.

An easy way to demonstrate the efficiency of nature's barriers, is as follows: break two whole eggs into two saucers. With one egg, mix the yolk and white together, leaving the other egg intact. Place both saucers on the windowsill. The egg left intact will gradually dry out, while the broken one will go bad very quickly.

# PROBLEMS WITH EGGS AND EGG PRODUCTION

## Thin-Shelled Eggs

Thin-shelled eggs are often associated with lack of calcium, lack of Vitamin D, overfat stock, inherited incorrect functioning of the reproductive tract, or pullets just coming into lay and heavy layers at the end of lay. Very rarely does the feeding of extra calcium have any effect, although the correct feeding of insoluble flint or granite grit will sometimes correct the problem. It will all depend on the cause.

## Separated or Floating Yolks

This is when the yolk breaks free from the chalazae or the chalazae breaks away from the shell. The yolk will then either float to the top of the shell or drop to the bottom. Once it adheres itself to the shell, the egg quickly rots. The cause is normally rough handling when collecting or at any other time, by the staff, producer, wholesaler, retailer or customer.

## Cracked Eggs

There are a variety of ways an egg becomes cracked, most of which are avoidable: insufficient litter in the nestbox, laying birds kept too long in lay, with shells becoming thinner, sudden panic in the poultry house or laying area, or eggs not collected frequently enough. Some of these cracks are visible. Very fine cracks which are not always visible are called hair cracks; the causes are those already mentioned. Hair cracks in fresh eggs are difficult to detect and are sometimes termed 'fresh or green cracks'. If there is a slight grey line on the shell, by applying a gentle pressure with two fingers at either end of the line, if it is cracked, the shell will open sufficiently to make it visible to the naked eye.

Another method is to tap two eggs together, if an egg is cracked the sound produced is dull against that of a complete shell. An experienced poultry producer. is able to tell by rubbing two eggs together in his hand. A few eggs are laid with a distinct ridge with crack lines. These are more likely to have been cracked in the uterus, with more shell deposited over the crack. They are unsaleable as first-class eggs as they are unsightly and sometimes break apart.

## Blood Spots

These can be detected only when eggs are candled, that is, placed over a strong light. When the egg is rotated the blood spot will show up usually at the side of the

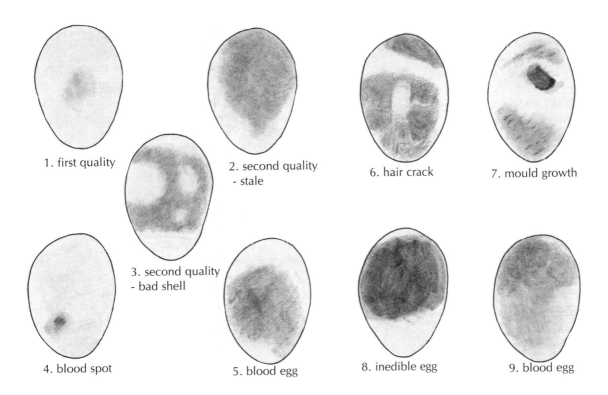

1. first quality

2. second quality - stale

6. hair crack

7. mould growth

3. second quality - bad shell

4. blood spot

5. blood egg

8. inedible egg

9. blood egg

*Egg faults.*

yolk, although it may be in the white. It is due to the rupture of a small blood vessel in the ovary. Such eggs are more common when birds are at the peak of their production, as at that time the ovary is being well nourished by the bloodstream. A sudden fright with ensuing panic may also cause this condition in a few eggs. Eggs with blood spots are completely edible but should not be sold. It appears that a few birds can be prone to producing eggs with blood spots and if traced to an individual, the bird should be culled. A very high protein ration can also be a contributory factor.

## Blood Eggs

When blood eggs are candled they give off a reddish glow, and when opened, blood is found to have intermixed with the albumen. On cooking, the white will become black, and the recipient may think they have an egg with a dead chick in it. The cause is due to the rupture of a large ovarian blood vessel. The reason is the same as for blood spots.

## Meat Spots

Meat spots are usually degenerate blood spots, or they may be caused by a small piece of tissue being torn from the oviduct and included in the white. These eggs are edible, once the offending meat spot has been removed. Causes are the same as for blood spots.

## Bad Eggs

Owing to some abnormality, such as a twist or tumour in the oviduct, the egg may be held up in the body of the bird for a considerable period. Due to continuous pressure or other causes it is suddenly released and laid. When candled, it will look black, and if held to the nose will smell rotten. Such eggs are rare, but it is possible to have a bad new-laid egg.

## Blood Rings

This is experienced only when a cockerel is running with the flock. On candling, a blood ring appears round the yolk signifying it is a fertile egg which has started to incubate in storage at a temperature of 20°C (68°F) or higher. It has died because the temperature was not sufficient to continue the incubation. All eggs, whether fertile or infertile, should be stored at an average temperature of 10–12°C (50–55°F).

## Odours and Smells

It is very rare for an egg to be laid with an unpleasant odour or taint. In nearly every case, if not all, the objectional taint has been absorbed through the pores of the shell. There are many reasons for this type of egg, from dirty nestboxes to collecting eggs in feed buckets, or placing them in smelly storage containers, keeping them next to strong-smelling feedstuffs, or petrol/diesel-fumed car boots, in fact any strong-smelling surroundings. All these will add up to fishy-flavoured eggs. Most egg taints occur with eggs kept in the fridge alongside strong-smelling food, onions, meat, cheese and so on.

## Discoloured Yolks

These are normally due to a feed problem.

Certain weeds such as pennycress and shepherd's purse, if eaten by laying birds, will give rise to greenish-coloured yolks. Germinating acorns if consumed in quantity, will have a similar effect. Linseed meal does on occasions produce olive-green yolks. If discoloured yolks are a problem, a study of the pullets' food and eating habits should be made.

## Watery Whites

In a young pullet's egg the thick albumen is very thick and strong and the yolk stands up well in the frying pan. As the bird becomes older the thick albumen will lose some of its thick consistency. At or near the end of lay, the white of the egg no longer stands up well when broken out, but spreads all over the pan; this is called a watery white. There is another reason which effects this abnormality, and this is the infrequent collection of eggs during the hot weather, or the incorrect storage of eggs in too high a temperature (*see* paragraph on Blood Rings).

## Deformed Shells

From time to time freak eggs of various shapes and sizes are produced.
(a)   Double yolk eggs, which in the main will be produced by young pullets when they first come into lay, are caused by either two eggs separating from the ovary at the same time and joining into one egg, or one yolk partially falling into the body cavity instead of the oviduct's funnel, and later finding its way back, joining another yolk as it enters the oviduct.
(b)   Extremely small eggs, so small that they seldom contain a yolk are called cock or witch eggs. Instead of a yolk they may contain a fragment of tissue torn away from the ovary, or some other foreign body. As it passes down the oviduct it serves as a nucleus which stimulates the

internal mechanism to operate, and in turn produces a tiny egg. This normally occurs in new pullets, or hens at the end of lay.

(c) Soft-shelled eggs (eggs without a hard shell) are produced more commonly from young pullets commencing lay or older hens going out of lay. These occur when the egg descends through the oviduct so quickly that there is insufficient time for the secretion and deposition of shell to take place. On rare occasions it may be that a particular bird's shell gland is not functioning normally.

## Extra-Large Eggs

Extra-large eggs vary in size and are produced as odd eggs mainly from young birds coming into lay, or by older birds whose uterus has expanded more than is normal. In the case of young birds, it can be caused by reverse peristalsis, which forces the yolk back up the oviduct and, on reverting, the yolk will collect a further supply of thick albumen requiring an extra size shell.

Less common is for the egg to be formed before being put into reverse thrust. When this happens it collects further supplies of albumen and another shell. When the owner opens the shell another fully formed egg will be found inside, the only difference being that the initial egg will contain a yolk while the outer shell only contains albumen. The writer has experienced eggs up to 170g (6oz) in size, but this was more common many years ago at the time when hybrids were first introduced.

Many of the problems covered are those seen during the time of new pullets coming into lay, and will be self-correcting. The very complex structure of the oviduct means that abnormal eggs of one kind or another may be evident as the whole reproductive system gears itself up

to produce the unbelievable number of eggs a bird will lay over a twelve month period. To see this in perspective, place egg trays holding 300 eggs next to one solitary chicken to witness and comprehend the enormity of the feat.

## Badly Deformed Eggs

An injury to the isthmus or uterus is sufficient cause for hens to lay wrinkled eggs. Odd-shaped eggs or eggs with unusual shells are more frequently produced when birds have suffered from severe shock. It is common to find freak eggs after a heavy thunderstorm, low-flying fighters, foxes, dogs or other predatory animals.

If the flock starts to lay wrinkled eggs, then a respiratory infection may be responsible and qualified advice should be sought immediately.

*Misshapen egg.*

## Hygiene

To safeguard from cross-infection via the egg or bird, and to avoid any problem of taints, hands must be washed before any eggs are collected and between collections. Trays and other containers used must be meticulously clean, and as soon as possible after each collection all clean eggs should be placed in a cool clean storage area, away from any possible form of pollution. Dirty eggs should be separated from clean eggs immediately after collection, and cleaned before putting them back with the other eggs.

## Pituitary Gland

This gland is about the size of a grain of wheat and is situated at the base of the brain. It is divided into two distinct parts – the anterior and posterior lobes – and they each secrete different hormones. The anterior hormones come into action to stop production and apparently may encourage the laying bird to become broody, provided the right messages are stimulated in the brain. An increase of hormones from the posterior lobe induces increased egg production and is activated by light passing through the pupil of the eye. By increasing the birds' day length gradually by artificial means, production is improved and maintained.

In practice, it has been found that where no extra lighting is given to flocks of less than 25 birds, provided they are kept under good conditions of management, egg production can be partially maintained by increasing the protein in the ration by 5 per cent. This is because there is less stress in smaller flocks, due to a smaller peck-order structure.

Although production will be reduced slightly about the end of February, production as well as egg size will increase quite rapidly, and over the course of a twelve-month laying period egg numbers and egg size will be equal to, if not better than, those given extra lighting during the winter months. In conclusion, extra winter lighting need only be considered for flocks of 25 birds and over.

# MALE REPRODUCTIVE SYSTEM

Each healthy cockerel has two testes, or testicles, shaped like an elongated egg and creamy white in appearance. They are situated at the head of the kidneys and fixed securely to the dorsal wall. From each testicle is a tube leading to the cloaca, called the vans deferens. At the point each vans deferens joins the cloaca there is a small swelling called the seminal vesicle whose function it is to hold the sperm.

From these two areas, sperm is able to pass to the outside of the body. Unlike ducks, cockerels have no penis, but a small rudimentary organ is situated in the middle of the ventral portion of the transverse folds of the cloaca. It is because of the lack of penis that infertility problems occur with some heavily feathered breeds of poultry.

The only way to overcome this problem is to pluck a few feathers from around the side of the vent, on the cockerel as well as the pullet or hen. Any other obstacle, such as a build-up of faeces around or just below the vent will need to be removed to obtain a good mating.

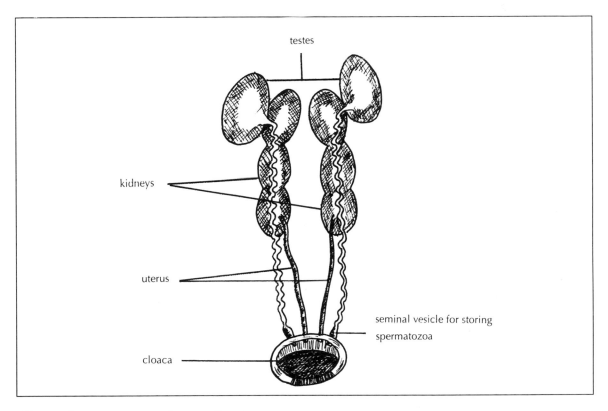

testes

kidneys

uterus

seminal vesicle for storing
spermatozoa

cloaca

*The male excretory and reproductive system.*

# 6 Natural and Artificial Incubation

## NATURAL INCUBATION

The production of chicks by a broody hen left undisturbed by – or even unknown to – the owner until she is seen trotting out from a secluded spot with a bevy of chicks trailing behind her, may seem to be an easy feat of nature to the observer. Many may feel that there is no point in studying literature which discusses the matter in detail. However, to become a successful breeder, the principles of incubation must be studied and learnt so that when problems arise they will be understood and corrected.

### Broody Hens

Consideration should be given to the most suitable hen required for successful natural incubation. Size and type of feather is of little consequence as hard-feather and soft-feather breeds can be equally successful. The weight can vary from the smallest of bantams to the heavy large fowl breeds. If small bantam or duck eggs are to be hatched, select broodies from the small lighter breeds. Normal-size hen eggs will benefit from an average-to-large hen, while goose eggs are better placed under large to very large birds.

Cross-bred hens are on average better broodies and mothers than pure breeds. Leghorns are the least likely breed to produce broody hens in any quantity and are notoriously unreliable. When crossed with Rhode Island Reds or Light Sussex, though, the progeny make very good broodies. Without doubt, the best cross is produced by using a Silkie cockerel on either large breeds or bantams. They tend to become broody at the drop of a hat, and will sit very tight. The breed or size of breed to cross with the Silkie cockerel will depend on the size and number of eggs required to be placed under each broody. The hens chosen are usually those already kept by the breeder, who will only need to obtain a male Silkie.

A few of our present-day hybrids will, in the right environment, become broody. It is not advisable to use them for this purpose as part of their broody instinct is missing, so these birds will not normally sit for the full period of time. If, during the early part of incubation a hen is clumsy and breaks eggs, then it is pointless to continue using her as she will also be clumsy with and possibly kill those chicks which eventually hatch.

The success of natural incubation, like artificial, depends on several important factors: the correct nutritional feeding of breeding birds, high standards of cleanliness, cool hygienic storage facilities, a basic knowledge of breeding, and the selection of clean quality eggs that are the correct shape and size. They should not be too small nor too large, and neither thin nor porous shelled, crinkly nor stale.

Before a fertile egg is laid, development

has already started by cleavage of the germinal disc. As a result of this cell division the germinal disc gives rise to a flat disc of cells known as the blastoderm. Its entire margin merges on to the yolk, from which it is separated by a small cavity.

When the egg is laid, providing the surrounding temperature is below 20°C (68°F), development ceases. However, if within a reasonable period the egg is brought to a suitable temperature, the arrested development proceeds.

It is important when using broodies to work out a timetable for setting eggs so that chicks will hatch on convenient days, and hatches will be spread to fit in with available housing for new chicks and growers, and that there are suitable available pens and houses for each and every hatch. If dates of hatching are allowed to clash, not only will more housing and equipment be needed but, depending on the size of the unit, too many growing birds of varying ages may be squashed together. This may lead to cross-infection between differing ages, which will subject these growers to a higher risk of disease and subsequent mortality.

## Sitting

When several broodies are sitting on eggs at the same time, eggs or newly hatched chicks can be moved about to compensate for birds going off brood and where too few chicks are hatched under individual birds. If fertility is found to be poor when testing on the 18th day, it is perfectly feasible to reduce the numbers of broodies by placing the eggs of one or two under the remaining birds. If the use of only one broody is anticipated, try to have a back-up bird to cover every eventuality.

When a bird becomes broody in the poultry house, do not leave her there in the hope that she will sit contentedly. She may, but other laying birds in the poultry house will lay eggs in the same box, which are then mixed up with the eggs already set. Although her eggs can be marked for easy identification, she will have to be disturbed each time the eggs are collected, which may cause her to become fed up and desert them. When she comes off to feed, it is possible her way back to the nest will be blocked by other birds laying, in which case she will sit in another box leaving her own eggs to become cold, killing the unborn chicks. Alternatively, she may end up sitting on too many eggs, some of which will become cold. As they become too many for her to cover, the embryos in these eggs will chill and die.

To make a suitable nestbox for broodies, a box or series of boxes measuring 30.5 × 30.5 × 30.5cm (12 × 12 × 12in), with a lift-up lid at the front, one per division, provides an ideal unit. The base can be either made from wood, or covered with 1.25 × 1.25 × 1.25cm (½ × ½ × ½in) wire mesh; this will protect the bird, eggs or newly hatched chicks from unwelcome rodents. On top of the floor place a grass turf which covers the whole of the floor area. Having cut the turf, turn it over and scoop out the centre (see diagram). Turn back, with the grass uppermost, and place it in the broody box. The centre will sink to represent a natural hollow in the ground. Cover with a 5cm (2in) layer of soft broken wheat straw or hay. When the eggs are placed in the nest they will naturally roll to the centre, preventing any eggs from being pushed accidentally to the side and chilling as the broody reshuffles the clutch. Some people like to place stones on top of flat turf in the corners to keep the eggs in the centre.

Delouse all broodies before they sit on eggs, and leave a dust bath containing delousing powder for them to use when they are taken off the nest to feed.

Before placing any fertile eggs in the box, place instead two or three pot eggs,

1   embryo after 24 hours incubation

2   after 36 hours incubation

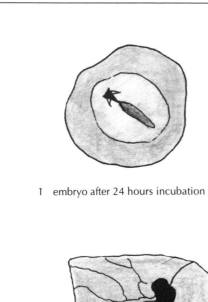

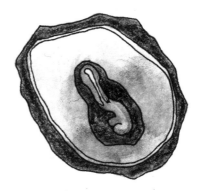

3   after 48 hours incubation

4   after 72 hours incubation

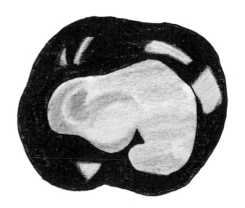

5   embryo chick fourth day

6   eighth day

*Evolution of the embryo.*

7 twelfth day

9 fully developed chick ready to hatch at 21 days

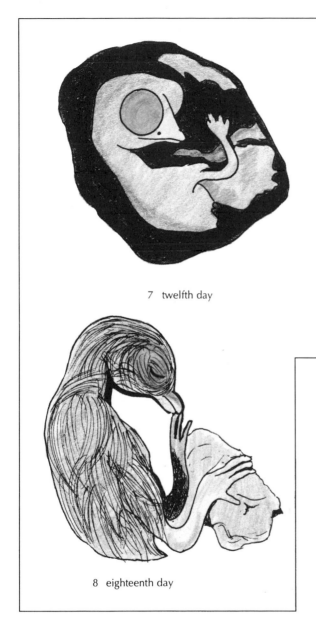

8 eighteenth day

feed. Take her off each day at about the same time; do not just open the front in the hope that she will be hungry and come off naturally. Some broodies at the beginning will sit very tight and not come off to feed or drink of their own volition, gradually starving to death.

A broody hen should come off her eggs every twenty-four hours, at which time she must be fed and watered. If she is able to run with the other birds she will have the opportunity of eating food which is available to other hens. Layers' mash or pellets are totally unsuitable for a broody hen because they pass through the digestive system too quickly, causing her to defecate on the eggs and soil the nestbox. During the period of incubation (21–22 days) broody hens will require a ration of mixed corn, made up of 15 per cent cut maize and 85 per cent clean whole wheat.

An average-size hen will cover between twelve and fourteen normal-size hen eggs. Do not put more eggs under her than she

to give the broody a chance to settle down overnight. If in the morning she has still not settled, replace her with another bird. When satisfied that the bird has settled and is sitting tightly, take out the pot eggs and replace them with hatching eggs when she is taken off the nest for her first can cover. This can easily be double-checked by gently placing a hand under her after she has settled for a few hours to feel if the eggs are all the same temperature.

Broodies turn their eggs several times a day, and as they do so they secrete a cleaning antibacterial fluid through the pores of the breast which cleans them and kills any harmful bacteria.

On the eighteenth day, when the broody comes off for her daily feed, collect the eggs in a tray and take them away to be candled. Take out all infertile eggs, also those with a partially formed embryo. Put back only those that have a good chance of hatching, before she returns to the nest. (If eggs are not candled the producer is unable to tell how many will hatch, and will keep the hen on newly hatched chicks for too long while waiting in vain for infertile eggs to hatch.)

Provided the shed the broody or broodies are housed in maintains a reasonable temperature in the winter, above 12°C (55°F), the turf will provide and maintain sufficient humidity up to the eighteenth day. After this and until the eggs start to chip, flick a little soft warm water directly over the eggs each time the bird comes off to feed. In late spring or early summer when temperatures have risen, the extra water is not necessary or recommended.

## Hatching

Once the eggs have started to chip, the broody will not want to come off the nest, and she should be left from now on until the hatch is complete. The period of time that she will sit without feed and water for this last stage is 48 hours. This is why, when they are all hatched, the chicks should be placed snugly in a warm box and taken into another room to allow the broody to feed, drink and possibly dust bath in peace. As soon as she shows interest in returning to the broody coop, gently carry her to her new broody coop, placing the chicks underneath her. Close the front of the coop, and give her time to settle with the chicks in the dark for thirty minutes to an hour. In the run immediately in front of the coop place a small drinker containing fresh water and a chick feeder. Once you hear the hen quietly talking to her brood, open the front of the coop to allow the chicks to feed and drink. The front of the broody coop is fitted with bars approximately 5cm (2in) apart, sufficient space to allow the chicks through but not the hen. The broody can then reach between the bars to encourage them to feed, but is unable to upset and scratch the feed over the floor and, in the same way, is restricted from tipping over the water fount.

Enclose chicks in a wire run to protect them from predators, especially from birds of prey such as magpies, jackdaws and crows. If the broody is to be kept in the same box in which the eggs were hatched out it should be thoroughly cleaned out, including taking out the turf and replacing it with fresh clean soft wheat straw or wood shavings. On no account use mouldy straw, because there is a risk that the fungi spores will be ingested into the lungs, causing death from Aspergillosis. The broody hen will not at this stage require an adult ration, the chick feed will help boost her strength after over twenty-two days of semi-starvation.

# ARTIFICIAL INCUBATION

The incubation period for a hen's egg is 21 days, but with artificial incubation the period is often slightly longer, except when the temperature of the incubator is too high. In this case, chicks will hatch out a day or two earlier, and take longer if the

*Eggs of various breeds for setting.*

temperature is lower than recommended by the manufacturer. Under identical conditions, eggs from light breeds hatch out slightly earlier than heavy breeds. Bantam eggs set in the same incubator as hen eggs will generally hatch out a day earlier.

The quality of eggs to be set has already been covered in the chapter on Breeding, but it is important to remember that to obtain the best hatching results, you must candle all eggs before setting. This eliminates the use of defective eggs enabling the incubationist to set a maximum number of quality hatching eggs.

Store eggs for as short a time as is economically possible. Eggs set the same day that they are laid will not hatch; they must be allowed to cool over night. Store them in a windowless or darkened room away from draughts and sunlight. Draughts cause evaporation, reducing the permeability of the shell's membrane. Eggs can be stored in sealed boxes and, if they are to be kept for longer than three weeks because a certain number of eggs from a particular breeding pen or individual hen is required, seal these eggs in plastic bags to prevent evaporation, enhancing their chances of reasonable hatchability.

## Incubator Housing

It is a very common failing that, having possibly spent a great deal of money for a new incubator, little thought is given to constructing an incubator room.

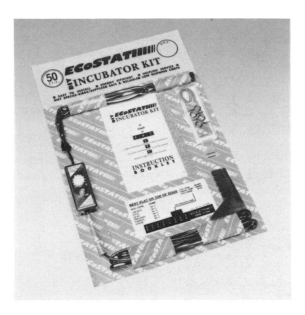

*An Ecostat DIY incubator kit.*

Incubators are found installed in garages, sheds, greenhouses, spare rooms, in front of windows and in school corridors. Whichever incubator is chosen and however expensive is of little consequence unless it is properly housed. The incubator room must be able to hold a fairly constant temperature, varying by only a few degrees. Large variations of temperature prevent the maintenance of stable conditions in the machine. It is not a question of maintaining a constant heat within the incubator, it is more complicated than that, because every change in temperature affects ventilation and humidity.

The ideal room temperature for a natural draught incubator is 15.5°C (60°F), and 21°C (70°F) for force draught incubators. It is not always possible or viable to construct such a perfect room, but it may be feasible to divide off and insulate a small area in an outside shed.

For winter hatching, consideration should be given to the installation of a small efficient heater run in conjunction

with an accurate thermostatic control unit, also installing at the same time a small ventilator inlet. To construct or convert such a room for incubation need not be costly, but will be very rewarding in improving hatchability. By the same method it is possible to construct a valuable egg storage unit.

## Natural Draught Incubators

Natural draught incubators are those where all the eggs are set at one level. The term 'natural draught' is really a misnomer, as direct draught will kill the living embryo. Air is taken in through small ventilator holes at the base and muffled to spread it evenly under the eggs, at the same time mixing with the heat produced from either an element fixed to the lid of the incubator or, as with older machines, with heat produced outside the cabinet and guided via a tube up and into the lid. The hot air is baffled by a layer of hessian as it is drawn down into the incubator. Small ventilator holes

*An Ecostat polystyrene incubator.*

*A ten egg automatic incubator.*

which are situated at the top of or the top side of the incubator, release stale air and at the same time control to some extent the machine's humidity.

The perfect temperature inside the egg is 38°C (100°F). With natural draught the temperature under the eggs is cooler than above. Therefore, to attain the correct temperature within the egg the thermometer should be placed or hung just above the fertile eggs. The standard recommended temperature is approximately 39.7°C (103°F), varying slightly with different manufacturers' designs.

This type of incubator is still used widely and very successfully. It has very few working parts to go wrong, the mechanism is easy to understand and simple and cheap to maintain, it is reliable and, in general, cheaper to purchase than force draught incubators.

Older models incorporated a hatching tray below the setting tray. The setting tray was shorter at the front and, as the newly hatched chicks dried out, they were attracted by and walked towards the light coming through a narrow window in the door. Moving as far forwards as they could they automatically stepped off the front of the setting tray and fell down on to the nursery tray below, where they cooled off, and were unable to interfere with, crowd or soil the remaining eggs.

On the morning of the 22nd day, all the strong healthy chicks will be ensconced in the nursery tray, and from there should be placed in a warm box and put under the brooder unit. Most modern incubators which include a hatching tray are not designed to cope with a natural transfer of chicks from one tray to another. As a result, chicks that hatch early take up too much space, soiling remaining eggs not yet hatched and crowding on top of late hatchers, possibly reducing the total hatch by a small percentage. This can be a problem when infertile eggs are not taken out on the 18th day, or when there are very few infertiles to take out. Nowadays hatching trays are designed solely for transferring fertile eggs to, after candling.

If during incubation there is a power cut, place a thick blanket over the incubator to keep eggs as warm as possible until the power is back on. If during the day the incubator breaks down or the power goes off unnoticed, provided the eggs are still even slightly warm the embryo will not necessarily die, but be a day late in hatching.

## Force Draught Incubators

In this type of incubator there is usually more than one level of setting trays, so to attain an even temperature throughout, a small capacity fan is required. The fan is used to circulate the warm air to maintain a constant temperature throughout the incubator. This then enables the incubator to be run at the same temperature as that required by the egg, approximately 38°C (100°F), which is lower than a still air or natural draught incubator. The running temperature varies a little from one manufacturer to another but this is clearly stated in the instructions.

Room temperature also plays an important part as can be seen in the table below.

The advantage of force draught incubators is that there are no restrictions as to the total egg capacity they hold. Capacity is only restricted by the size of incubator purchased along with the manufacturer's recommendations. The larger the capacity the higher and wider they are, rather like a cupboard with several shelves, taking up very little extra space. Using a multi-tiered unit allows the owner to set eggs every one or two weeks, maintaining a steady flow of chicks, at the same time as setting fresh eggs.

At the eighteenth day the corresponding trays are taken out and, after candling, fertile eggs are placed in a hatching unit away from the setting machine. The now empty trays can be filled with a further supply of fertile eggs, after being thoroughly disinfected. Place newly filled trays at the bottom of the incubator and move the others up towards the top. By adopting this system, the uppermost trays will be the next to be taken out for hatching, so that if the internal temperature varies, i.e. a little cooler at the bottom than the top, all eggs set will experience the same differences and hatch times should always be consistent.

There are incubators which incorporate the incubation and hatching in the same machine. The hatching section is only large enough to take a third of the incubator's total capacity so hatching is staggered. The remaining eggs which are possibly at two different stages of development suffer because;

| Room Temperature | Incubator Temperature |
|---|---|
| 4.5°C/40°F | 40.5°C/105°F |
| 10.0°C/50°F | 40.0°C/104°F |
| 15.5°C/60°F | 39.5°C/103°F |
| 21.0°C/70°F | 38.8°C/102°F |
| 26.6°C/80°F | 38.3°C/101°F |

*A Curfew incubator model 250 which can have inserts for game eggs.*

(a) A higher level of humidity is required from the 18th day until the hatch has been completed, and this may prove injurious to the embryos of eggs which have been set more recently.

(b) During hatching a large amount of debris from newly hatched chicks circulates in the incubator blocking, in the process, the pores of other eggs.

(c) There is little chance of properly cleaning out the debris to reduce to a minimum the risk of cross-infection on the shells of the remaining eggs. An amazing amount of filth builds up during hatching and this should be cleared immediately after each hatch.

There are available on the market fumigators which can be used to disinfect the incubator containing eggs at any stage of development, but it is not good practice to rely on fumigators to solve problems brought on by poor incubation techniques.

## TURNING EGGS

In the natural state, the hen will shuffle her eggs many times a day and, because of this, it is necessary when turning eggs by hand to turn them at least three times every 24 hours. It is even more advantageous to turn them more frequently, such as five or seven times. But unless retired or working from home this is rarely practical; it is more the norm to turn them only three times. The most effective way of carrying out this operation is to turn the eggs at eight-hourly intervals or as near as possible, commencing at approximately 7 a.m., the second turn 3 p.m. and the last 11 p.m. Select the turning periods to suit each person's individual availability.

To ensure that each egg has been turned correctly when setting, mark a cross on one side and a nought on the other. This will ensure that each individual egg has been turned the right half turn. When turning by hand, take out the centre eggs each time and place them in the outside area to ensure that all eggs during the period of incubation will receive an equal temperature and be protected from being kept in a 'dead spot', should one exist.

Most incubators now have fully automatic turning incorporated and the owner has only to check daily, by noting the position of the trays or eggs that the turner is continuing to operate.

In general, automatic turners with just one level of eggs roll the eggs from one side to the other as in hand turning. This operation is so slow that it is very difficult to detect with the naked eye. When

*A Brinsca 91cm (36 inch) Hatchmaker handturn.*

setting eggs, mark a few with noughts and crosses, to be certain no breakdown in the turning has occurred. In other machines, eggs are placed point down instead of being laid on their sides and are tipped from one side to the other. Note the tray's position each time a temperature reading takes place and enter on the record chart.

Each time eggs are turned manually record the temperature before lifting off the lid, and record the temperature each time the automatic turner is checked. It is far better to over-record than not record at all. It is only in this way that hatches can be improved.

Eggs need not be turned after the 18th day; the automatic turner must be disengaged before replacing fertile eggs after their final candling.

## EGG CANDLING

In general, hens eggs are tested for fertility on the 18th day. They may also be tested on the seventh to eighth day to check the air sac, which by its size will suggest whether water needs to be added, and the quantity of infertile eggs that can be withdrawn.

The easiest method of candling eggs is by using a small candling box. It can either be home-made or purchased from an incubator retailer. The size of a home-made wooden candling box is 10cm wide × 20.5cm long × 15.5cm high (4 × 8 × 6in). One end, wired to a bayonet socket, must be detachable so that a 40 watt light bulb can be fitted, and which can be changed to a 60 watt if very dark-shelled eggs are to be tested. Cut out an egg-shaped hole two-thirds the size of a 57g (2oz) egg on the top

*A Curfew Autoturn electric incubator.*

of the box to rest each egg on when testing.

When candling eggs at an early stage lay them on the box over the aperture and quickly rotate; any impurities are then visible as they float with the turning yolk. At the latter stages of incubation the egg is turned slowly to check for deformities.

If there is any doubt as to whether to take an egg out, mark it with a pencil and check to see if it or any other marked eggs have hatched. The embryo at the final stage of testing is not always as clearly defined as many incubation books would have the reader believe. The only positive way to learn and build up confidence is to take a chance, marking eggs and carefully recording the results.

Where several trays of fertile eggs are to be checked, then these can be candled reasonably efficiently by mounting each

tray in turn on to blocks running the length of the tray and, with one hand holding a strong torch, gradually moving it to and fro under the eggs. The other hand is able to take out all the clear eggs, together with those where it is obvious that the embryo has died at an earlier stage.

## COOLING AND HATCHING TIME

It can be argued that each time the hen comes off her eggs to defecate and eat, the eggs are cooled and, because of this, eggs set in incubators should also have periods of cooling. It is often forgotten that although the incubator is designed to replace the broody hen it is purely a machine, and cannot possibly copy the

INCUBATOR CHART.

DATE SET. _____                    TIME TEMP UP. _____

| DATE | 1st TEMP | 2nd TEMP | 3rd TEMP | MAX MIN | BREEDS | NO.SET | INFERT | LEFT IN | NO HATCH | % |
|---|---|---|---|---|---|---|---|---|---|---|
| SET | | | | | | | | | | |
| 1 | | | | | | | | | | |
| 2 | | | | | | | | | | |
| 3 | | | | | | | | | | |
| 4 | | | | | | | | | | |
| 5 | | | | | | | | | | |
| 6 | | | | | | | | | | |
| 7 | | | | | | | | | | |
| 8 | | | | | | | | | | |
| 9 | | | | | | | | | | |
| 10 | | | | | | | | | | |
| 11 | | | | | | | | | | |
| 12 | | | | | | | | | | |
| 13 | | | | | | | | | | |
| 14 | | | | | | | | | | |
| 15 | | | | | | | | | | |
| 16 | | | | | | | | | | |
| 17 | | | | | | | | | | |
| 18 | | | | | | | | | | |
| 19 | | | | | | | | | | |
| 20 | | | | | | | | | | |
| 21 | | | | | | | | | | |
| 22 HATCH | | | | | | | | | | |

REMARKS DURING INCUBATION PERIOD.

DATES WATER ADDED AND HOW MUCH.

*Incubator chart.*

instinctive techniques of a hen. It cannot copy the natural cooling period when the broody comes off to feed, nor does it move eggs about, equating the amount of heat each one receives. It is the incubator's ventilation system that has been arranged to compensate partially for nature's way of cooling.

After the final fertility check, and having filled the water containers with the necessary amount of water, the incubator should be closed and not opened again until the morning of the 22nd day. Under no circumstances should the door be opened or the lid lifted to check the state of the hatch or to take out chicks which have hatched out early. By opening any part, the internal environment is destroyed along with the humidity, and many unhatched chicks are prevented from coming out by a dried membrane sticking to their down, thus preventing them from revolving inside the shell to cut their way out. If for some reason or other it is important to interfere with the hatch, have a bottle of warm water available with a spray top to wet all eggs as soon as the incubator is opened. This will prevent dehydration of the remaining eggs. (The relative humidity in still air and forced air incubators is 60 per cent.)

## DISINFECTION OF INCUBATORS

Incubators which are used for setting and hatching must be dismantled and thoroughly cleaned out between each hatch if the incubator is used solely for setting eggs which are moved on to a hatcher at a later date. If in continuous use, the incubator should be fumigated each time eggs are removed and again each time new eggs are introduced. There are one or two products on the market which have been specifically designed for this purpose. Hatcher units must be dismantled and thoroughly cleaned between each hatch. To miss out fumigation at the appropriate times allows harmful bacteria, which are always present, to build up and eventually partly or fully destroy the hatch. Always make sure that all airways are free and brush off each time any 'down' collected on or over heaters.

## INCUBATING OTHER SPECIES

For those species of fowl which need an incubation period of more than 21 days, eggs will need to be checked for fertility and moved to the hatcher 4 days before they are due to hatch. Japanese Quail, on the other hand, need only be moved 2 days before hatching.

| Periods of Incubation | |
| --- | --- |
| Species | Total Days |
| Large fowl & bantams | 21 |
| Ducks | 28 |
| Geese, small breeds | 30 |
| Quail, Japanese | 16–17 |
| Pheasant | 23–24 |
| Guinea fowl | 28 |
| Turkey | 28 |
| Muscovy | 35–37 |
| Geese, large breeds | 33–35 |
| Quail, bobwhite | 23–24 |
| Partridge | 23–24 |

# 7 Nutrition and Digestion ————————————

The feeding of livestock is the most important factor concerning their welfare. To rely on hearsay, which may be made up of a series of old wives' tales, or take advice from other ill-informed sources, many of which are from people who have kept poultry for only a few years without ever researching the subject, is no doubt the biggest problem the beginner and semi-experienced person has to contend with. Without adequate amounts of a correctly formulated diet no animal is able to function properly, least of all a hen. Where incorrect feed practices are involved, the bird's resilience to disease is reduced and vices such as egg eating, feather pecking and cannibalism will occur.

Correct feeding must fulfil four basic functions:

1 Provide the right material for growth.
2 Give energy to keep the body functioning efficiently.
3 Create material to produce new tissue and to replace worn out tissue in the course of living.
4 Produce eggs, meat and spermatozoa.

The above functions are satisfied by feeding a complete ration, and such a ration must contain the six following substances:

1 Proteins
2 Carbohydrates (starch, sugar and fibre)
3 Fats and oils (either extract)
4 Mineral salts and minerals
5 Vitamins
6 Water

## PROTEINS

These are a complex group of organic compounds consisting of carbon, hydrogen, nitrogen and usually sulphur, phosphorus and iron, but the presence of nitrogen is the most characteristic feature of proteins. They are body-building foods necessary for growth, maintenance and production. Proteins are said to contain approximately 16 per cent nitrogen and, in order to calculate the protein present in any substance, the analyst first estimates the nitrogen content and then multiplies this figure by 6.26. The result is rarely very accurate because all the nitrogen may not be present in the form of protein. This is therefore expressed as crude protein and it is the crude protein which is printed on the bag label, not the available protein.

The accuracy of this figure will depend to a great extent on the constituents included in each manufacturer's formula. It is this variance of materials by manufacturers that can be misleading to the producer and, because of this, egg production or fattening performances will vary from one brand of feed to another. By law each brand has to have affixed an analysis of the feeds and the contents printed in decreasing order below. There are cases where the crude protein printed on one label is 2 per cent lower than another, yet the lower one may contain a higher available protein which is more beneficial to the hen and production will be improved.

An old, yet sound, system used by poultry farmers to assess the ability of a food, was to keep changing manufacturers over a period of time until a suitable feed was found for performance. Once this had been achieved, then the producer remained loyal to that feed company's products. This method is still adopted today by some who doubt the quality of an existing ration. It is however, detrimental to the birds' welfare if various brands of feed are changed at the whim of the producer, be it for cost or convenience. This is because each firm's ration will vary in texture, and if the texture of a specific feed is not so palatable to the bird, consumption drops, followed quickly by reduced egg yields. This will also affect weight loss in fattening cockerels.

## CARBOHYDRATES

These form a very large diverse group of feeding stuffs which consist of carbon, hydrogen and oxygen. The hydrogen and oxygen are always present in the same proportion as in water. Carbohydrates are divided into two groups, one soluble and the other, in the form of fibre, insoluble. The soluble carbohydrates are broken down into simple sugars and absorbed to provide energy. If there is too much present in the system the excess is stored as fat. Fibre is of no use as a food, and indeed if too much fibre is present in the ration it will affect the digestibility of that ration.

It has been found that rations which include more than 10 per cent fibre have a detrimental effect but, on the other hand, an inclusion of fibre up to 7 per cent

opens up the feed, giving it the required texture to make it palatable. Palatability is extremely important to the feeding of the bird and should the feed be ground too fine then the bird will not take in sufficient food to maintain itself. It may even stop feeding altogether on a specific manufactured feed. The grist (coarseness) should be such that the wheat in the ration is cracked and not milled. One should be able to recognize most of the main ingredients by the naked eye.

## FATS AND OILS

Whether one or the other is used is really of little importance as both contain the same elements as carbohydrate, although containing a much greater proportion of hydrogen and oxygen. The digestive juices break fats/oils down into glycerine and fatty acids, yielding between 2.1 to 2.5 times more energy than the equivalent weight of carbohydrate.

## MINERAL SALTS AND MINERALS

Mineral salts will be present on the manufacturer's label as 'Ash'. To find out the amount of mineral present in a feed, a proportion of the feed is measured and placed in a suitable container and heated until the feed is reduced to ash. From the residue the percentage of minerals is calculated and, when analysed, it will be found to contain calcium, potassium, sodium, magnesium, manganese, iron and traces of zinc and copper, together with silicon, sulphur, chlorine and phosphorus. A bird will require many of these minerals during its life, the majority of which are only required in minute quantities and these are referred to as 'trace elements'. They are not normally added to the diet but are part of it as they are to be found in the other ingredients.

## Minerals

Calcium and phosphorus form the greater part of the skeleton and egg shell. Minerals also form part of the tissue and muscles and are necessary to maintain muscle tone and correct the pressure of various body fluids. Poultry keepers are often encouraged to feed excess oyster shell, sold separately or mixed with insoluble grit. This is encouraged by many pet shops and cash and carry retail outlets, especially if a producer is complaining about too many weak or soft-shelled eggs.

*A wellington boot converted to a grit hopper.*

With the knowledge feed manufacturers have today, feeds are formulated to include the correct balance of calcium and phosphorus to maintain a layer at 80 per cent production for several months. It is mistakenly thought by some that to avoid soft-shelled eggs, additional oyster shell is required. This practice can result in the completely opposite effect.

A calculation known as the calcium phosphorus ratio was established many years ago. The ratio is made up of 1.1 per cent calcium to 0.7 per cent phosphorus. If there is an excess either way it may give rise to perosis (slipped hock tendon found in chicks), rickets or soft-shelled eggs. This is because both appear as tri-calcium and, if there is too much of one, it will be excreted in conjunction with the other (calcium phosphate), until only one of the properties remain, producing a complete imbalance. If, however, a glut of soft-shelled eggs is experienced and it is not due to feed or respiratory diseases, feeding hen size flint or granite grit it may for some reason correct the problem.

# VITAMINS

It was established many years ago that rations which included proteins, carbohydrates, fats and minerals were not sufficient in themselves to produce good growth, production and vitality. To achieve this, vitamins had to be added. All birds kept on genuine free-range conditions (that is, where all birds are able to go out each and every day) require fewer vitamins, but where birds are kept intensively or semi-intensively extra vitamins need to be added.

## Vitamin A

This vitamin is found in fats of animal origin. A deficiency of this in a bird's diet causes leg weakness, general unthriftiness and white pustules in the mouth and throat. The kidneys become enlarged and pale due the collection of urates in the tubules. Apart from the bird suffering from nutritional roup, the deficiency lowers the bird's resistance to disease. Vitamin A is known as an anti-infective vitamin. Birds on range cannot secure it from feeding off plants but it is available from feed containing carotenoid pigments such as maize, alfalfa and carrots, which birds are able to convert into vitamin A. Synthetic sources are now used in most of today's rations.

## Vitamin B Complex

B1, B2, B6 and B12 which include folic acid, pantothenic acid, nicotinic acid, biotin and choline, are all responsible for high egg and meat production. They can be included naturally in a ration via yeast, the outer coating of grains and, to some lesser extent, green vegetables.

Birds kept on good pasture and given a light feed of grain in the afternoon will have an excess of this vitamin, although a winter ration for breeding birds will require extra amounts. Where this is not practised, hatchability is reduced with some embryos dying during incubation. It is also responsible for curly toe in young chicks, although this can be genetic or caused by uneven temperatures during the incubation.

## Vitamin D

Calcium and phosphorus, which form the bone structure, require this vitamin to be able to calcify; it also assists in the hardening of egg shells. This is absorbed by direct sunlight on extensively kept flocks. Another rich source for birds during the winter months is cod liver oil. Infra-red heaters are a good source of D3 for young

and growing chicks reared under electric infra-red brooders. The absence of the vitamin D3 results in poor egg production, brittle bones, leg weakness, and poor and brittle feathering. Birds kept in a windowed house on deep litter will not reap the benefit of sunlight through glass windows as glass prevents the important ultra-violet rays from penetrating.

## Vitamin E

Although too much can cause sterility, insufficient amounts will lead to poor hatchability, with embryos dying during the first 3 to 4 days of incubation. Extensively kept poultry will find a sufficient supply from grass and wheat.

## Vitamin K

This is always included in a well-formulated ration. Lack of it causes haemorrhage in the breast, legs and other parts of the body. The problem when trying to clear rats or mice from a feed store where they have access to poultry feeds, is that Vitamin K being a coagulant, acts as an antidote to most mouse and rat poisons.

## General

In many, if not all, cases of stress, a course of soluble vitamins in the drinking water for 5 to 7 days will help a bird or flock back to health, without relying too heavily on today's array of antibiotics. Antibiotics are invaluable when used correctly, but should never be used as standard treatment, as unfortunately witnessed in many small animal veterinary practices.

# WATER

Water is the most important factor of any

diet for all poultry, animals and humans. It must be supplied on an adlib basis, clean and fresh each day. Water forms the major part of the body, is essential for natural body functions and, if limited, the first effect is a depletion in egg or meat production and, secondly, severe dehydration leading to high mortality. It is well documented that man can live for a far longer period on water than on food; this is also true of birds and other animals.

# PALATABILITY

This has to some extent already been covered, but it is important to understand more fully what part palatability plays in the birds' eating habits. If the texture of the food is too fine, birds have difficulty in swallowing and reject it. By watching carefully as birds feed one can see the bird picking up and continually rejecting unpalatable food. Wheat, for example, is very palatable, and given the choice they will eat their fill of wheat in preference to a more suitable balanced diet. Barley is coarse and rejected, the evidence seen growing in the pen the following year. Pellets are palatable and one could be excused for thinking that these are more readily eaten than a coarse grist layers' mash. In fact, given the choice, the birds prefer mash to pellets. If birds have been reared on a pelleted food they are quite happy to continue doing so even when offered mash, but if the change over to mash is gradual and after a time they are given the choice, it will be found that their preference is for mash.

It has been known for producers, albeit small, to mix wheat or mixed corn with pellets or mash to feed as a once-a-day dual ration. The problem here is that the wheat, being more palatable, will be consumed first, and production suffers as a result of such a low-protein intake. If wheat or mixed corn is to be fed, the latter consisting of 15 to 25 per cent cut maize, it should not be given any earlier than mid-afternoon, and then at the rate of no more than 28g (1oz) per bird per day. An afternoon cereal ration consisting of whole wheat, cut maize, whole barley and whole oats should be avoided. Whole barley is unpalatable and whole oats are of very little nutritional use to the bird, being basically fibre. Where birds are reared on range during the late spring to early summer months they tend to become precocious because of natural increasing daylight hours, resulting in young birds coming into lay as early as 14 to 15 weeks of age and producing very small eggs, with the possibility of increased mortality because of pullets prolapsing.

To prevent this happening, the experienced rearer will feed a whole-wheat diet from 12 weeks of age onwards, the lower protein (11 per cent) to avoid early maturity. If, on this diet, growing pullets continue to mature too quickly, then whole oats is substituted for wheat as a bulk food. When feeding any low-protein diet careful watch must be kept on the growing birds because, should they become stressed in any way by fright, disease or are generally off colour, their feed must be changed immediately back to a well-balanced grower's ration.

There is always the question of whether to feed pellets or mash. A day's ration of pellets can be consumed in half an hour, but it will take a bird about three and a half hours to consume a day's ration of mash, provided it is fed continuously. Birds fed on mash normally split up their feeding times with other interests and necessities, and are therefore much more fully occupied than those given pellets. The pellet-fed bird exhibits aggressive behaviour leading to feather or vent pecking, cannibalism, and egg eating, etc. Pellets also leave birds bored, especially during the winter months when during prolonged periods of high winds and/or rain/ they congregate in groups in and around the poultry house. It is here where many harmful vices begin. Pellets are used by some because they are deemed less wasteful than mash. This only happens when using the wrong type of feeders, or suitable mash feeders incorrectly adjusted.

Pellets are manufactured by grinding mash into a fine meal, and with the addition of a binder such as clay, the pellet is formed. Problems of excess dust in pellet feed many occur during periods of inclement weather, poor manufacture or too much rough handling between the mill and the customer. This dust is completely inedible and wasted.

Pellets are used by some for feeding on range in order to avoid using feeders, in the mistaken belief that birds have little need of troughs, consuming whatever is scattered. If one were to look very carefully on the ground a short time after feeding, then the waste of uneaten food would be observed.

## FEEDING AND MOULTING

Feathers and skin structures during moulting must be nourished. Moulting is a process of shedding old feathers and growing new ones. Chicks moult four times during the growing period and adults approximately once a year or, more accurately, between laying periods. The first period of lay may last for up to two years under good management. Both poor and heavy layers take 6 to 7 weeks to moult out, although the break in production is normally between 8 to 10 weeks. The difference between slow and rapid moulters is that the latter renew a greater number of feathers over the same period of time. Generally speaking, the best layers will continue to lay eggs throughout the period of moult, although not as many, while the majority of hens will cease to lay altogether. It is important to continue to give a high-quality layer's ration to support the bird throughout the period of moult.

A bird's feathers represent 6 per cent of the bird's body and 15.2 per cent of the total energy required. To change to a whole-grain feed over this period to save money is bad for the bird and false economy.

## EFFECT OF FOOD ON MEAT POULTRY

In Great Britain the general public requires a white-fleshed bird. This is primarily a breed characteristic. Breeds such as the Rhode Island Red, which normally put on yellow fat, can, if given suitable foods which exclude such pigments contained in yellow maize, grass meal or other green food, be made to deposit white fat and so produce a reasonably white-fleshed carcass.

## EFFECT OF FOOD ON EGG QUALITY

Consumers demand well-flavoured eggs with deep-coloured yolks. Yolk colour is greatly affected by the type of food the birds receive. Materials such as yellow maize, grass meal and other green foods produce the desirable orange/yellow yolk. Carotene converts vitamin A, xanthophl does not, paprika given at the rate of 4 per cent of the ration will produce brick-red yolks. The yolk colour is due to capsanthin which has no nutritive value. Certain weeds, such as pennycress and shepherd's purse, eaten in quantity will be responsible for greenish-coloured yolks. Acorns produce olive-green yolks.

The common colour agents used in rations these days are as follows:

**Canthaxanthin = Carophyll Red** Used as a red pigment in layer's rations. It is mainly used as a synthetic but it also exists naturally in certain crustaceans.

**Citranaxanthin** Synthetic version used as a red pigment in a layer's diet.

**Capaxanthin** A natural substance of paprika, used as a red pigment.

**Lutein & Zeaxanthin** Natural source taken from marigolds. Used as a yellow pigment in a layer's diet.

**Carophyll Yellow = Ethyl Ester or Beta–Apo 8 = Carotenic Acid = Lucantin Yellow** Synthetic and used as a yellow pigment in a layer's diet.

**Butylated Hydroxyanisole = BHA or Ethoxyquin** These are anti-oxidants. The purpose of an anti-oxidant is to preserve the vitamins in a diet.

**Alpha Tocopheral = Vitamin E.**

**Cupric Sulphate** A synthetic source of copper, necessary in a poultry diet.

**Sodium Selenite** A synthetic source of selenium.

**Sodium Bicarbonate = Bicarbonate of Soda** Used to supply sodium without increasing the salt in the diet.

**DL Methionine: Synthetic Amino Acid** This amino acid is essential for feather and bone growth, and lysine affects egg size.

**Prairie meal = 60% Maize Gluten** A natural yellow colourant. Lucerne and grass meal are also used for the natural pigmentation of the yolk.

**Kemglo Products** Based on marigold and paprika, natural colourants.

All feed bags by law must have the contents printed on the bag or, more commonly, on a label affixed to each bag.

## A MERCHANT'S LABEL ANALYSIS

The label description illustrated (opposite) is for an additive-free free range layer's ration. The contents are normally stated in descending order by weight. Always look for the 'best before' date.

**Note**: The above details are only a guide, manufacturers will vary their rations according to availability. Always store feed in a cool dry room/shed. Protect from vermin. Never place bags containing feed directly on a concrete floor no matter how dry you may think it is. Keep off the floor by placing it on wooden boards or slats.

## THE DIGESTIVE SYSTEM

Poultry are considered the worst converters of protein of all farm animals; this is because they have a very simple digestive system.

The bird's beak, made up of an upper and lower mandible, is perfectly suited to picking up small objects. A bird will use its beak much the same as a dog uses its nose: it picks and rejects objects which are not considered palatable. It spends a considerable time pecking at hard surfaces, presumably to ascertain whether they are edible, trimming their beaks in the process. Poultry keepers know to their cost the painful pecks they experience on their legs and feet as hens crowd round in a welcoming and friendly manner.

To cat grass or other similar vegetable matter, the bird pecks and breaks off manageable lengths with a sharp jerky action, taking it to the back of the throat with the aid of an arrow-head-type tongue. The tongue also assists the swallowing of mash/pellets and corn. Very little, if any, digestion takes place in the

| Oil<br>% | Protein<br>% | Fibre<br>% | Moisture<br>% |
|---|---|---|---|
| 4.1 | 17.0 | 7.0 | 14.0 |

| Vit. A<br>iu/kg | Vit. D3<br>iu/kg | Vit. E<br>iu/kg | Copper<br>mg/kg |
|---|---|---|---|
| 8000 | 2400 | 12 | 23 |

Methionine: 0.28%

Merchants Serial Number – – – – – – – –

Best before/Vitamins present until end  month/year

Ration Ingredients [in descending weight order]
Wheat, Wheatfeed, Sunflower Meal, Limestone Grit,
Peas, 60% Maize Gluten, Beans, Lucerne, High Energy
Fat, Soya, Minerals, Hipro Soya, Vitamins.

mouth, although amylase has been found in the mouth's saliva. Amylase is an enzyme which converts starch and glycogen into sugar called maltose. An enzyme is a digestive ferment produced in small quantities by a living organism capable of breaking down large quantities of a specific substance, without undergoing any change itself. All feed is taken through the digestive tract by means of involuntary rhythmic contractions of the gut called peristalsis.

Food once at the back of the throat is taken down the gullet/oesophagus into the crop, where it is stored and softened by secretions from the mouth, gullet and crop. When the food is sufficiently soft it automatically passes on to the small glandular stomach/proventriculus, which is well supplied with secretory glands, and at this stage the gastric juices are added. The gastric juices contain hydrochloric acid and pepsin, whose action it is to break down proteins.

Food now passes on to the gizzard, which is a large and very muscular organ, whose main purpose is to grind down feed with the help of insoluble grit. This increases the feed surface, preparing it for later absorption. Without the aid of insoluble grit in the gizzard it is nearly impossible for a bird to make any use of whole grain and hard cut cereals found in a good coarse-ground layers' mash, as it passes unground through the digestive tract. No digestion takes place in the gizzard, although a small amount of gastric juices are passed on from the glandular stomach.

From a healthy functioning gizzard, a very fine powdered food, already mixed with some liquid juices, passes into the duodenum, where it is attacked by the pancreatic juices which are responsible for the final breaking of the food constituents. The largest single organ in the body is the liver which produces bile, storing it in the gall bladder. The bile emulsifies fats which are then broken down by enzymes. Food passes through the small intestine and on to the large intestine. The small intestine is five or six

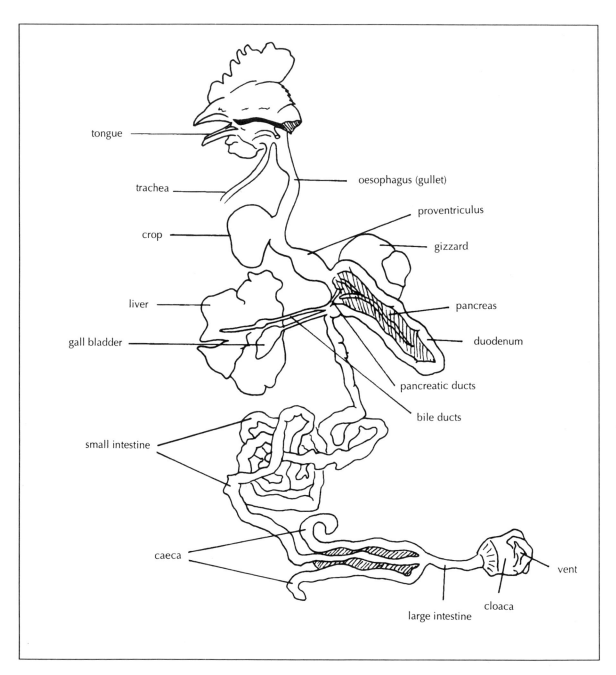

*The digestive system.*

times the length of the bird and is where most of the food is digested. The whole internal area of the intestine, from the duodenum to the cloaca, is covered with innumerable projections called 'villi'. These enormously increase the surface area and it is through these that the now liquid feed is assimilated and carried by the bloodstream throughout the body.

At the point where the small intestine meets the large intestine are two blind guts called 'caeca'. These two blind guts are more of less filled with faecal matter. The function of the caeca is concerned with the digestion of fibre and absorption of water from the faeces.

The last part of the digestive tract is the large intestine (rectum), which is concerned with the absorption of water from the urine as it arrives via the ureters that are attached to the kidneys. These urine solids are excreted as the white part of the faeces.

The cloaca, which is the part that lies immediately inside the vent, is the area or chamber which is the common pool of the digestive tract collecting the products of the kidneys and the genital organs and also houses the muscle which controls the opening and closing of the external orifice.

There are two kidneys which lie embedded in the bony recesses on each side of the vertebrae. Each kidney has three lobes receiving blood from the renal arteries and returning it cleaned to the renal veins. The kidney's function is to take from the blood all waste products which are collected and stored in the ureters, where it is finally discharged into the large intestine, and the remaining water is reabsorbed back into the body through the intestinal wall.

# 8 Rearing Pullets for Egg Production ——

To obtain the best production, maximum disease resistance and low mortality, the most critical period of a bird's life is during the rearing stage. An attempt to cut costs by feeding cheap and unsuitable food together with generally poor management are detrimental to the bird's health and future production. However good the genetical breeding is of hybrid, first cross or pure bred, it will be unable to produce eggs efficiently if poorly reared.

## NATURAL BROODING

Once the broody hen has hatched out her full complement of chicks, these chicks will need to be taken away from her to give the hen time to feed and drink and possibly dust bath. She cannot do this with her new young chicks cheeping continuously in her hearing. The coop designed to transfer mother and chicks to should already have been thoroughly cleaned and disinfected several days previously in anticipation of the hatch. Clean white wood shavings make an ideal material to use as litter, but only 2.5–5cm deep (1–2in).

Make or buy a coop 60 × 60cm square × 45cm at the front, dropping away to 30cm at the back (24 × 24in × 18in high at the front by 12in at the back). Fix vertical bars or dowelling at the front to restrain the hen for the first few days, setting these 5cm (2in) apart, and making the centre bar removable to give the broody hen

access after the first five days' restriction.

Place the hen in the coop as soon as she shows signs of settling down after her feed, reintroducing her to the newly hatched chicks by placing them gently beneath her, darkening the coop for the next hour or so. Place a small drinking fount in front of the broody coop together with a feeder. Take the cover off the front of the coop to allow the chicks to drink and feed away from the hen's feet; at the same time, she should be able to reach through the bars to encourage them, and also be able to eat and drink herself. There must be a small run attached to the coop to protect chicks from other predators.

After the first five days allow the broody hen out with her chicks, giving her and them more space to roam. How well it is necessary to protect them at this stage will depend on their accessibility to predators, including those on the wing. Chicks may be kept with the hen for up to six weeks of age; after this it is advisable to separate them, putting them in a small rearing house and run, and returning the hen to the flock.

During these early stages of rearing, and until they are eight weeks of age, chicks must be fed ad lib on a chick starter ration. Give the hen during her period with them a handful of mixed corn each evening to ensure she settles down for the night with a full crop. She spends most of the day encouraging them to feed and brooding them, especially during the first few weeks. She is, therefore, unable to feed herself to her full capacity on dry

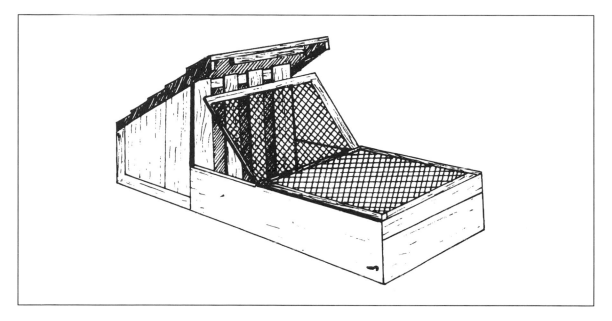

*Brooding coop.*

chick food alone. A hungry bird becomes restless at night and this can result in chicks being trodden on in the dark.

At eight weeks of age the young growing birds should be changed on to a grower's ration, but make this change-over a period of four to five days by mixing the chick and grower's ration together. Day-old chicks are born with a high level of immunity to disease, and when reared under a broody hen their immunity level quickly rises, provided the coop is regularly cleaned and broody and chicks moved to fresh grass each day. This is the main advantage they have over chicks reared under artificial heat.

Young growing birds must not be put with older birds until they are at least 18 weeks of age. Do not put in less birds than those already housed in the laying pen and provide them with an extra feeder, otherwise the established hens will keep the young birds from feeding properly, causing unnecessary stress. Where possible, house different ages, however mature, in separate houses and runs.

## ARTIFICIAL REARING

The majority of chicks reared on a relatively small scale are reared under infra-red heating elements, and large numbers under gas canopies. In both instances chicks can be easily observed both day and night.

When using an infra-red element, it is preferable to use one that does not emit any light, called a 'dull emitter'. Using the old-fashioned red or white light infra-red elements gives growing chicks constant light, encouraging early maturing, as well as feather pecking and other vices. The element that gives off a strong white light is worse than the red because if a chick damages itself accidentally or is pecked, the wound, if it bleeds, will attract all the other chicks to attack it. Red lighting makes blood appear black, so helping to reduce the possibility of further attacks.

The dull emitter gives the owner some control over lighting patterns, such as a ten or twelve hour day during the growing

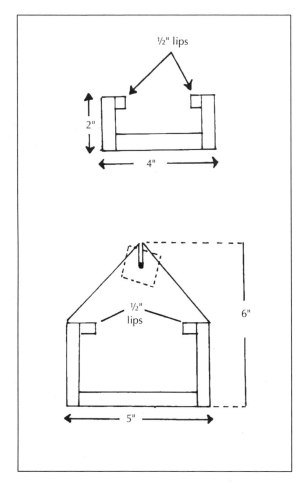

*Mash hoppers for (a) chicks up to one week old and (b) chicks for one to five weeks old.*

period. Birds without strong light throughout the night are less nervous, settling easily and quickly once the lights go out. If the rearer is worried that when the light is turned off chicks are unable to find their way back to the heat source, a small 15-watt red pigmy bulb may be fitted near the ceiling and kept on overnight.

Cover the floor of the brooder house with 7–10cm (3–4in) of clean white wood shavings, and for the first 5 days fit a circular surround around the brooder lamp. A surround can be made from corrugated cardboard, or better still 60cm (2ft) high hardboard. Buy 2.4 × 1.8m (8 × 4ft) sheets of 6mm (¼in) hardboard and cut lengthways; four lengths joined together is sufficient for up to 250 chicks. The sheets are joined and held together by making very large clothes-pegs. To make a peg, cut off a 60cm (2ft) length of 4 × 4cm (1½ × 1½in) sawn wood and cut lengthways in half. Join together at the top using a 15 × 4cm (6 × 1½in) spacer between the two sections.

Suspend the brooder heat unit over the centre of the surround 38 to 46cm (15 to 18in) above the litter. The reason for the variation in height is that it takes into consideration room temperature and breed of bird. Apart from the obvious distinction between bantams and large fowl, some breeds of large fowl require different temperatures. Give the new chicks a full half hour to settle before making any adjustment to the brooder height. If the chicks are huddling together and standing on tiptoe at the centre of the brooder, they are too cold and the brooder will need to be lowered. However, if they are well spread out in a circle away from the heat source, they are too hot so the brooder will need raising. Ideally, chicks should be evenly spread under the heat with a little clear area at the centre about the size of a cup's diameter. Minimum room temperature for the first week should be between 18 and 24°C (65 and 75°F) and thereafter reduced to approximately 15.5°C (60°F) by the fourth week.

The heat of the brooder should not be relied on to warm the brooder room. Far too many chicks are lost through dehydration because of cold room temperatures. They find it too cold to feed or drink properly and give up. The breeder may be blamed for selling small weak chicks, but dehydrated chicks shrink and are constantly cheeping loudly until they die on the sixth to seventh day. They are

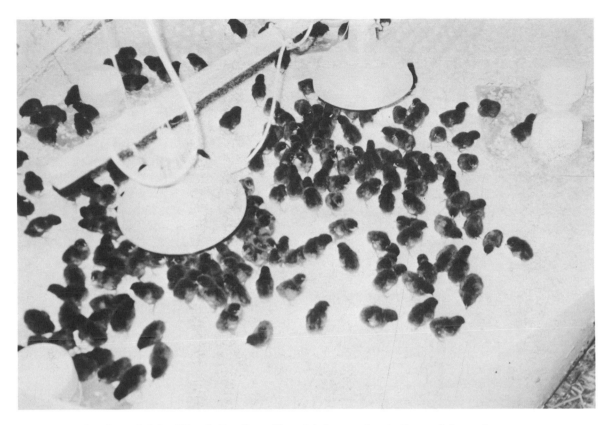

*One hundred and fifty Black Rock pullet chicks under infra red brooders.*

seen huddled and protesting with two or three little wing feathers sticking outwards away from the body.

Switch on room and brooder heat the day before chicks are due to arrive so that the wood shavings are warm and dry. Place drinkers and feeders around the perimeter of the brooder the previous evening so that the water has had the chill taken off. Those people brooding chicks artificially for the first time may wish to place a thermometer on the litter under the centre of the heat element, which should read in the region of 35°C (95°F). This temperature is a guide only when setting up and, once the chicks have been gently placed under the brooder, it should be taken away and the brooder height adjusted according to how the chicks are spread beneath.

A further thermometer (maximum/minimum) should be hung on the wall, not too high; and be read and recorded twice a day, a.m. and p.m. The most important time to check the height of the brooder is after the chicks have settled for the night when it is easier to observe any alterations that are necessary. If the chicks have been startled by the operator entering the brooder house it is not possible to make any alterations until they have settled again.

To start with, place adequate drinking founts around the brooder, putting the feeders slightly further away. Chicks must be able to find the water quickly, the feed they will find as they venture past the drinkers. Do not expect them to eat much for the first three days but from the fourth day on, their appetite will start to increase quite rapidly.

Chicks which have been in transit for a considerable time should be individually 'beak dipped'. To do this, place each beak into a cup of water with the chill taken off, to ensure it has its first drink before placing under the brooder. This method may be time consuming but is well worth while, forestalling early mortality caused by dehydration.

## Drinkers

The old-fashioned bottle drinkers have been replaced by a variety of various-sized plastic drinkers. These all work on the same principle as the glass bottle, controlled by vacuum. When selecting a new plastic drinker, look for those which are designed to prevent chicks from perching on the top and soiling the water. The larger plastic and galvanized founts can also be used provided there is sufficient floor space. A guide to water requirements is as follows:

### Per 100 Chickens

4.5 litres (1 gallon) water daily 1st week
7 to 9 litres (1½ to 2 gallons) daily to 6 weeks
13.64 (3 gallons) daily to 10 weeks, and thereafter 18 litres (4 gallons) daily

## Feeders

During the first 5 days it is good practice to allow a certain amount of wastage to make sure all chicks are able to eat to their full capacity. As they become stronger, then any wastage should be avoided. Clean out all waste food from the brooder area especially if it has become damp. Keyes trays are often used

for the initial 5 days, after which they should be removed and burnt. The base of the large plastic tubular feeders can also be used from day one where a large number of chicks are reared together, and where the area to start with is sufficient, as these take up a great deal of space.

Where possible, try to purchase feeders which prevent chicks from perching or walking on the top and messing in the food. The two designs which protect feed being fouled and wasted are troughs with a central spindle, or hanging tubular feeders, provided that the height of the latter is adjusted on a regular basis. The correct height is where the bottom of the base is a little above the top of the smallest bird's back, and in this way no valuable floor space is lost.

### Calculation of feeding space per 100 birds

Day old – 2 weeks   in line 2.4m (8ft) = 1.2m (4ft) trough
2–4 weeks   in line 3.7m (12ft) = 1.8m (6ft) trough
4–8 weeks   in line 6m (20ft) or 2 tubular feeders
8–12 weeks   in line 7.3m (24ft) or 3 tubular feeders
12–18 weeks   in line 9.2m (30ft) or 3 tubular feeders
From 18 weeks   in line 12.2m (40ft) or 4 tubular feeders

Each day move the water and feed a little further away from the brooder until they are as near as possible to the circular surround without obstructing the actual perimeter. On the morning of the sixth day take away the surround, giving the chicks the whole of the brooder house area to run in. During the first day without the surround chicks will make a considerable noise cheeping. Ignore this, but check that they are all under the brooder at lights

*Mixed breeds at one week old.*

out. During a hot summer it may be that a few small groups will form well away from the others; provided they seem well settled, leave them. If they do become cool during the night they will move in towards the heat. In the larger brooder house it may be beneficial to install red pigmy lights directly over the heat source to guide them under.

If the rearer were to take the trouble to sit on a chair in the brooder house after the lights have gone out and observe their reactions it would be seen that those on the outer edge of the brooder, as they cool down, move into the centre by running over the backs of the others, and those who have become too hot move out. This movement will continue throughout the night. It is therefore vital that there is sufficient room for the chicks to get away from the heat to allow natural feather growth. Those people who attempt to brood chicks by trapping them in large cardboard boxes or metal baths, rather than construct a suitable rearing unit, will produce birds uneven in size that are backward and with poor feathering, plus possible disease problems at a later stage.

Provided young birds are kept in a warm well-ventilated room, it should be

*Four-week-old Cream Legbar, Dorking, Light Sussex and Welsummer chicks.*

possible to turn off the brooder when they are about five to six weeks of age. Allow a further two weeks cooling period before moving them to an outside unit on range. If they have to be moved at an earlier age, it is advisable to have an alternative heat source handy should the weather become cold and wet. At eight weeks, growers should be changed from a chick starter ration on to a grower's mash or pellets. It is advisable to change the diet before putting the birds out so that stress is kept to a minimum.

## Rearing on Range

Young birds must be put on fresh grass or land which has been rested for at least three to four weeks, having been liberally limed during the interim period, and the house thoroughly cleaned and disinfected between each batch. They must be kept separated from older growers and away from mature birds to avoid cross-infection and stress. Where there are several ages of birds kept on a farm or smallholding, the operator must always service them (feed and water) from the youngest to the oldest. In this way, any faeces picked up on boots will be transferred only to older birds whose immunity system is stronger than that of various ages of younger growers. The operator who looks after the youngest chicks, reared on the floor in the

*A good, deep-bodied layer.*

*The head of a good layer.*

brooder house, is well advised to have a different pair of shoes or wellingtons to put on before entering. This will help to prevent many problems, including coccidiosis, which can be introduced via older birds' faeces carried in underfoot, at a more concentrated level than the anti-coccidiastat included in the feed is able to give protection against.

When young birds are to be reared on range, the rearer must provide adequate protection against the elements for young and older birds alike. Wind and rain shelters should be provided, otherwise during inclement conditions birds will tend to stay in the house or hang around the immediate outside perimeter. When this happens, growers become bored, and may resort to feather pecking and other vices, while at the same time soiling the outside area to such an extent that there is a greater risk of disease outbreak. Furthermore, this area will need resting for a further 12 months before siting other growers on the same land.

Always encourage birds away from the house by placing the drinker at the bottom of the pen, and if grain is fed in the afternoon, scatter it in different areas of the run each day to encourage them to make use of the whole area. Provide a monthly supply of hen-size grit in a heap in a different area of the run each time, about 30g (1oz) per bird. This will help prevent the gizzard from becoming impacted with an excess of fibrous material, such as grass.

Try to keep the grass in the pens short, but if the grass has grown too long between batches, it is better to leave it long than cutting it just before the birds are put out. This is because if long lengths of grass are left on the ground, growers and mature birds who are unable to break off small pieces, will, by swallowing these dry or semi-dry leafy blades of grass, suffer and die from impaction of the crop or gizzard.

## Poultry House for Growers

There are two main types of outdoor poultry house, one with a solid floor and perches and the other with a slatted floor. When using a house with a perch system, do not fit the perches until the growers are about 12 weeks old. If they are introduced to perches before this age, there is a risk that several will developed crooked breasts due to young growers' breast bones not being fully calcified. This injury will not affect egg production, but birds with this deformity should not be selected as possible breeders. This is because at the time of selection the breeder may not know for sure whether the deformity has been caused by early perching or is a genetic problem.

Slatted floors are a very good and labour-saving system of housing as they help prevent the possibility of death by crowding if birds are frightened at night by foxes or other predators. Young birds during the growing period are nervous and vulnerable to panic, more especially during the period of rehousing. With a slatted-floor house the ventilation is normally even, reducing the risk of dead spots (stale-air pockets), and birds reared in this way seem to be stronger, healthier and less susceptible to disease.

## Prevention of Disease

To help keep disease to a minimum never allow friends, visitors, potential customers or officials on to the rearing site. If a vet is to be called then they must wear protective clothing, washing in disinfectant, before use and immediately after use. No officials, whoever they represent, should be allowed near any of your flocks without carrying out the same procedures as your vet.

### Rearing Floor Area
0.1 sq. m (1 sq. ft) per bird to 18 weeks of age if reared intensively.
1.7 sq. m (2 sq. yd) per bird of grassed pen area to 18 weeks of age.

### Feed Consumption Based on 100 Chicks

1st week 4.536 kg (10lb) of feed, increasing by the same amount each week to the 10th week, then the rate is slowed down to an increase of 2.3kg (5lb) per week.

During the first 8 weeks on chick starter rations they will have eaten 175kg (7 × 25kg bags of feed), 360lb.

By the 18th week growing pullets will have eaten approximately 512kg (20½ × 25kg bags of feed), or half a tonne.

These figures are meant to be a guide only as amounts of feed used will depend on breed of bird and wastage. It is therefore very important to record amounts fed so that accurate costings can be worked out for each batch.

# 9 Rearing Heavy Birds and Preparing them for Table

There are two basic differences when rearing heavy table birds as against pullets for egg production, which are:

1 The requirement of a greater floor area per bird.
2 A different feeding programme.

Those considering this type of project will need to:
(a) Check possible market requirements.
(b) Check with the local Health Authority regulations concerning the killing and preparation for retailing direct to the public.
(c) Check if there is a local packing station willing to kill, pluck and eviscerate small numbers of birds, which is also cost-effective.

## HOUSING AND EQUIPMENT

### Floor Space

The UK Animal Welfare Code of Practice states that at any one time, the average liveweight of stock must not exceed 3.2kg (7lb) per 0.1 sq. m (1 sq. ft). This regulation would seem to have more to do with broiler production than with heavy table birds. It also does not take into consideration free-range-reared birds.

Acceptable floor space will vary throughout the world according to climate, breed of bird available and housing. It is important that when rearing heavy birds, there are sufficient in a house to maintain a comfortable temperature along with sufficient ventilation to assist in keeping the litter dry.

For heavy cockerels to grow evenly and fatten well when kept intensively, they should be stocked at a minimum of 0.3 sq. m (3 sq. ft) per bird. This provides adequate room for movement, allowing birds sufficient space to eat and feed without harming one another. It is also much easier to keep litter in a drier and more friable condition.

The area required for birds to be ranged should to some extent be controlled by the more limited movements of these heavy birds. There is no need to allow them more than 1.1 sq. m (12 sq. ft) per bird of free range covered by vegetation, with a house area of 0.1 sq. m (1 sq. ft) per bird.

### Feeding Space

In practice, it is advisable to allow 2.5cm (1in) extra per bird of trough space than for pullets. If tubular feeders are used, work on the basis of 20 fattening cockerels per feeder or 5 feeders per 100.

*Week old chicks under a gas heater.*

## Drinking Space

Cockerels require approximately 1.25cm (½in) per bird up to 8 weeks of age and 2.5cm (1 in) to killing. Water is important for growth rate, so there must always be a plentiful supply of clean fresh water available. As the cockerels increase in weight they become less eager to move around. For this reason it is important to make sure that drinkers are evenly distributed and not to rely on one central point.

## Litter

The provision of adequate litter in terms of quality and quantity throughout the growing period will have a profound influence upon the final profitability of a batch. The three main choices available are:

1  White wood shavings
2  Chopped straw
3  Shredded paper

Availability and cost have to be considered when choosing a litter, but other important factors concern scratchability and absorbency.

Chopped wheat straw makes a good litter bed, but is not always available and can be expensive. Shredded paper is dust

*Heavy broiler cockerel. (Photo courtesy of the Cobb Breeding Company Ltd).*

free and is a good absorbant material but better suited to growing pullets than fattening cockerels. The reason for this is that like all litter it needs to be turned continuously, and it has to be the bird that does this by continuous scratching. The cockerel is not very energetic, preferring to eat, drink and rest, especially as he gets older and becomes heavier. Shredded paper tends to stick and matt at the surface building up an ever-increasing coating of faeces, while the underside remains clean and undisturbed.

Wood shavings are easily turned by scratching, and are the most absorbent of the three materials, so keeping the bird's feathers clean while at the same time providing a warm insulated bed. Fattening cockerels should never be given the opportunity to perch because perching causes crooked breast bones and breast blisters, both of which make the bird unsaleable as a quality table bird. Woodshavings have a moisture content of between 14 and 18 per cent and are recommended at the rate of 600kg (11.8cwt) per 100 sq. m (1,000 sq. ft) on concrete or wooden floors.

Apart from the use of good litter, good management is essential to successful rearing, and from the beginning, the art is to create and maintain litter which is friable and free of wet patches.

## Feeding

There is a sound range of feeds available for the rearing of broilers on a large scale, but there are few feeds available for rearing heavy cockerels in smaller flocks. The only suitable birds to rear and fatten to such heavy weights are broiler breeds.

Because these are bred to make very rapid growth, the use of a correct feed is of the utmost importance. Broiler feeds on the whole are designed and manufactured to put on quick growth at an early age and also take into account the extra stress experienced with large flocks of growers kept intensively under one roof.

Small flocks kept intensively or extensively, which are given a greater amount of area per bird with an extended period of growth, will do far better on a less pushy ration. A sensible approach to feeding is to start them on a chick starter ration, the same as is fed to pullet chicks for the first six weeks. This will considerably reduce the problems of leg weakness associated with broiler birds. Young birds under a steadier growth regime have time to strengthen their leg muscles and joints before the upper body becomes too heavy. At six weeks of age they can then be changed on to a cockerel fattening ration or, if that is not available, an ordinary broiler grower pellet, until killing. There is no need for a broiler finisher ration, and they must not have a ration which includes additives such as an anti-coccidiastat during the last two weeks.

By using the suggested feeding programme the rearer can expect an average live weight of approximately 5.5kg (12lb) at 12 weeks of age. It is not advisable or economic to keep birds for more than 14 weeks of age for two reasons. The first is that after 14 weeks some of the more precocious birds will try to tread (mate) the others, causing ugly scratches on the back, damaged legs and general panic. Secondly, food conversion to meat makes it totally uneconomic.

## General

Uneven bird distribution, for whatever reason, can lead to reduced growth rates, poorer feed conversion and an increased variation of live weight plus poorer grading. The most common causes are:

(a) Poor ventilation resulting in inadequate circulation of fresh air.

*Broiler chicks under a gas brooder.*

(b) Cold spots caused by poor circulation.

(c) Irregular light intensities within the house.

(d) Inadequate water and feed distribution points.

(e) Wet litter caused by poor ventilation, insufficient drinkers or poorly adjusted automatic drinkers.

(f) Birds reared on range, muddy conditions surrounding the house, with house facing the wrong way, and insufficient or no shelter from wind and rain.

## COSTINGS

The following feed consumption rates are given as a guide only; they will vary according to the standard of management and general environment.

| | |
|---|---|
| 1 to 6 weeks | 3.3kg (7.3lb) |
| 6 to 14 weeks | 14.4kg (31.7lb) |
| Overall feed per cockerel | 17.7kg (39lb) |

Average live weight to 14 weeks of age is approximately 4.9kg to 5.4kg (11 to 12lb). The estimated weight loss after plucking and evisceration is approximately 15 per cent.

**Note** These figures are for males. Females give a better food conversion to meat, better meat to bone ratio and are smaller and ready a little earlier.

Purchasing as-hatched chicks will give the producer a satisfactory variation in weight and will prolong the killing time, females first, which can be an ideal arrangement for small-flock owners with limited labour.

## FLAVOUR

Type of feed plays very little if any part in producing flavour in the bird. It can affect the colour of the fat, especially when the ration contains a high percentage of corn (maize).

The production of a well-flavoured tender bird is achieved during the time between killing and evisceration. Birds which are killed and plucked one day, then left to hang a few days before evisceration takes place, will be both tasty and tender. During the hot summer months there is no need to hang them for more than one to three days, but during a cold spell they can be hung for up to two weeks. Oven-ready birds produced by the large multiple packing stations, where from killing to final evisceration and freezing takes less than half an hour, are generally tasteless and with a fibrous texture. It would be impossible for such plants to maintain a high standard of hygiene and viability if hanging time were allowed.

## PREPARATION OF BIRDS FOR THE TABLE

The correct procedure for killing and the preparation of hens and table birds is of the utmost importance to the small producer who cares for the welfare of his birds and at the same time is concerned about making the enterprise viable.

There are three basic options available to the producer:

(a)  To take old hens to market live and leave it to the purchaser to deal with the matter.
(b)  To sell them to a poultry packing station, although very few will buy small numbers of birds.
(c)  To prepare and sell table birds of either gender on site.

The A to Z of killing, plucking and final preparation of birds for the table is shown in picture form to make it easier for a beginner to understand.

Before any bird is prepared, it should be starved of feed and water for up to 24 hours.

 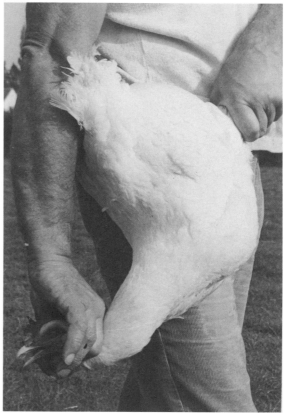

## Killing

1   Hold the bird firmly in the right or left hand, whichever you feel most comfortable with, and with your free hand take hold of the primary feathers of each wing, passing them to the hand holding the legs. Grip these feathers and legs together to prevent the bird from flapping, which can cause bruising or at worst a broken wing.

2   Slide the index and forefinger of the free hand down the neck until they are against the head. Quickly and firmly stretch the neck, at the same time pushing your knuckles into the neck vertebrae, and pull the head upwards into the palm of your hand. You will feel the neck dislocate.

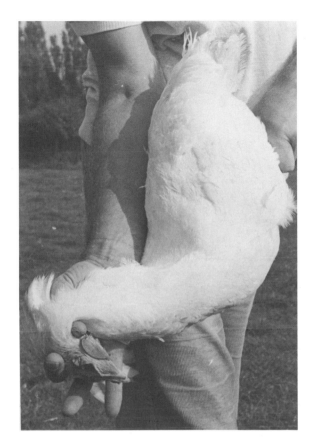 

3  As the neck dislocates, continue to stretch it over your finger, creating a gap of 5–7.5cm (2–3in). The purpose of this cavity is to collect the bird's blood as soon as it is hung upside down.

## Plucking

1  Still holding the wing-tips firmly, pluck all the primary, secondary and tail feathers, pulling down and away in the opposite direction of their growth.

2 Now concentrate on plucking the breast feathers, starting at the neck and working quickly up the breast again, pulling them against the direction of growth, towards the head. Several feathers can be pulled out with each movement, keeping the plucking hand close to the body. Don't pull outwards away from the body. If it becomes difficult or the skin is very tender, it may be necessary to pull out one feather at a time until the difficult section has been plucked. Always keep the skin in the plucking area tight. After the breast, continue on to the legs, the back, and finally the wings. Once the wings have been finished, fold them back.

3 Plucked birds are known as 'New York dressed', and a few people still like to buy their table birds at this stage. The chicken should be hung in a cool, dust and fly-free store, and just before hanging, squeeze out any fluids or faeces from the vent. If this is not done, this area around the vent will quickly turn green. Providing the store room is cool 10–12°C (50–55°F), the carcass will improve in flavour and texture over the next two to three days. New York-dressed birds used to be hung during the winter for over two weeks, but this is now internationally disapproved of.

4   Prior to oven-ready preparation, each bird will need to be singed to burn off surplus body hair, which can clearly be seen in the previous photograph. To do this, pour a small amount of methylated spirit into a metal lid and light it. Unfold the wings and turn the chicken gently over the flame, ensuring that all the body, legs and wings are singed. A long taper can be used as an alternative, although it is better to do this while the bird is still hanging upside-down.

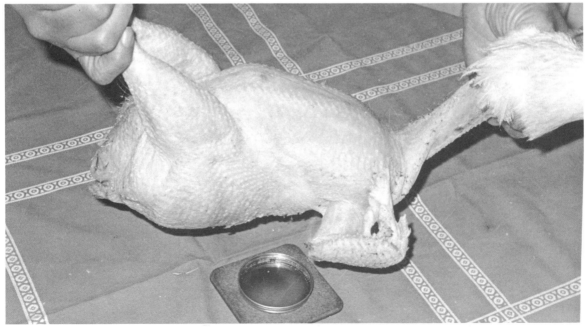

## Preparation for the Table

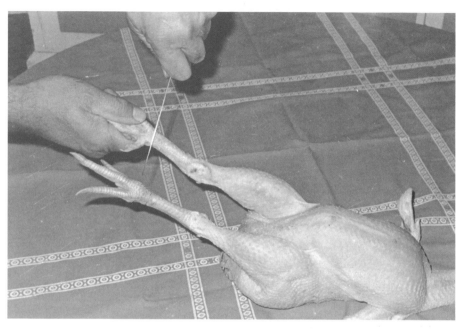

1 With a sharp knife, cut the skin around the base of the leg, just above the foot. Avoid cutting the sinews at the back of the leg.

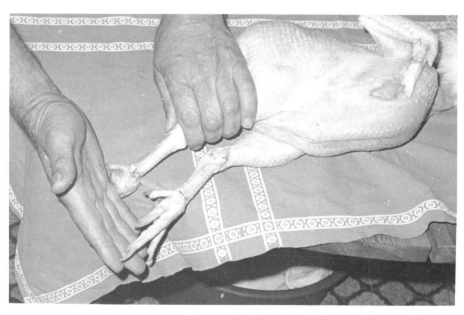

2 Position the leg over the edge of the table so that the cut is in line with the side, and a swift karate chop on the foot will break the bone. Now twist the foot so that it is left hanging only by the sinews.

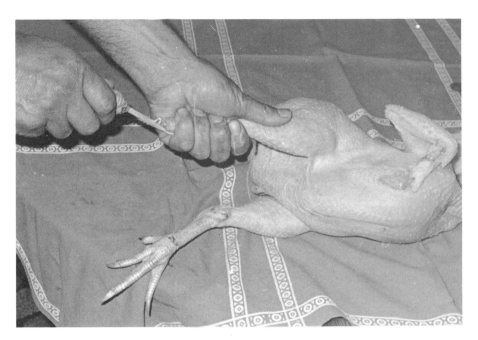

3 Holding the top of the leg firmly with one hand, pull hard and straight with the other hand holding the foot. The sinews will come away with the foot.

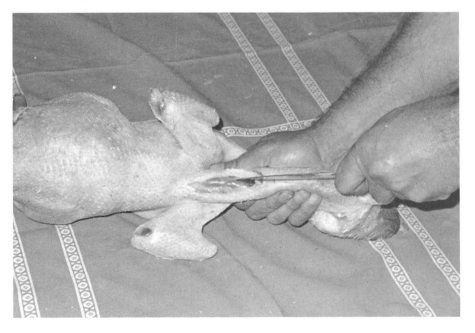

4 Hold the skin of the neck tightly in one hand, and at the same time cut the skin with a sharp knife from the base of the neck to the point of dislocation. Now cut off the head and dispose.

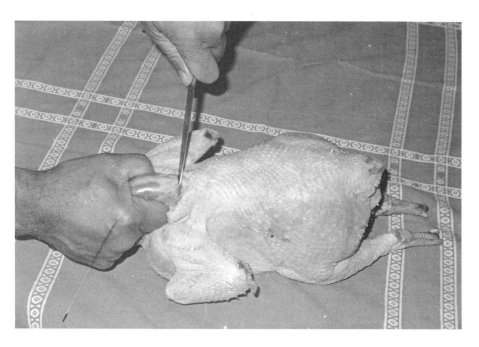

5 Free the skin away from the neck. Grip the neck and cut it off as close to the back as possible. It may be necessary to twist the neck as the cut is made.

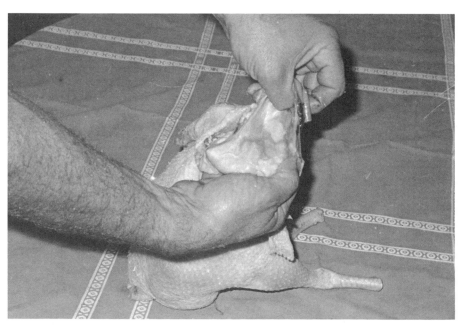

6 Sit the bird on its backside, hold the neck skin and peel away the crop, gullet and wind pipe (trachea), so all that is left is a nice clean section of skin.

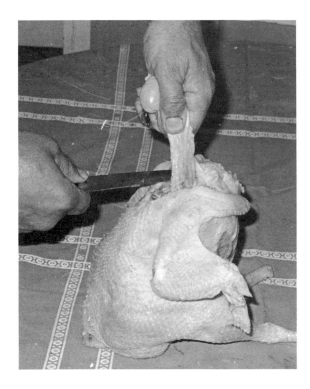

7   Pull both the gullet and wind pipe as far out as possible and cut tight to the body.

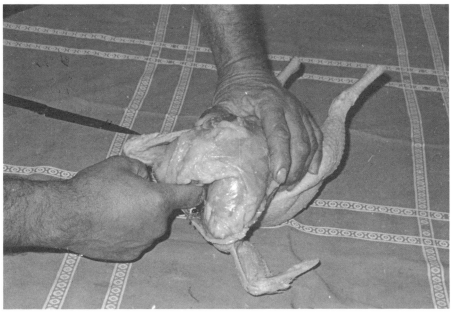

8   Lay the chicken on its back, stretch the surplus skin over the breast and insert the index finger into the cavity immediately above the neck stump. Work the finger round to free the lungs away from the rib-cage and then on up, freeing the heart and surrounding tissue.

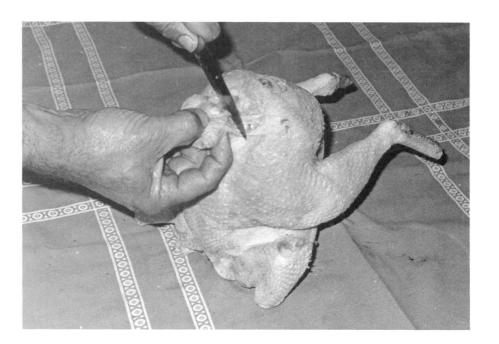

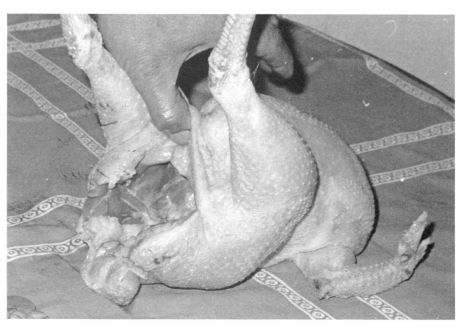

9    Turn the bird the other way up so that it is resting on the neck cavity. Holding the tail with the thumb and forefinger, cut down in towards the tail, not away from it. Make the incision large enough to push the index finger in, and once inside twist the finger to hook it round the large intestine. Slide the knife in, sharp edge away from the finger, and cut out and down. The result of this operation is that the intestine is left intact with the vent, and separated from the body.

118

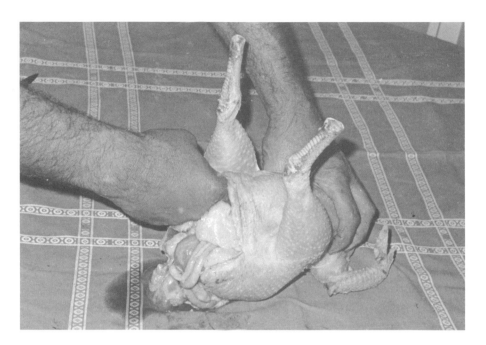

10    Enlarge the cut to enable the hand to enter the cavity, freeing all the membranes from the rib-cage and body.

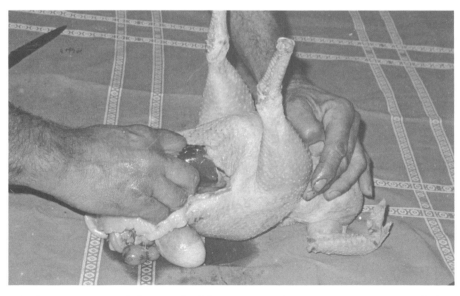

11   Once free, the whole contents of the body can be drawn out intact in one operation without breaking. If birds have not been sufficiently cooled, the testicles or ovary are sometimes left behind. These can be deftly removed with the aid of a knife, severing any remaining membranes. Check carefully that all parts, including the lungs, have been removed. Do not at this stage use water to wash out. Any surplus matter remaining should be wiped out with a clean cloth.

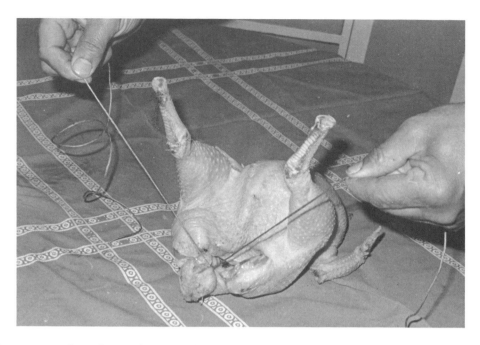

12   The carcass is now ready to be tied to make it look attractive and edible. If it has been tied tightly, then the breast will stand out well, attracting the attention of the potential purchaser. Cut off a 0.9m (3ft) length of string to commence tying the chicken. First, start by tying the tail (parson's nose).

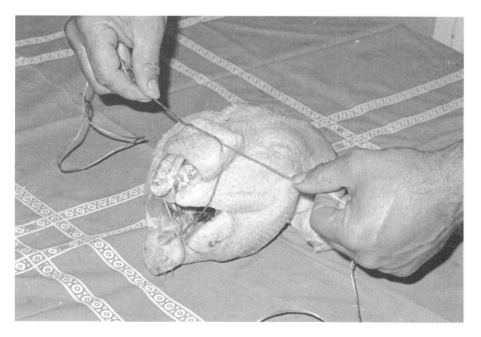

13   Tuck the legs into the body and tie tightly, but don't knot.

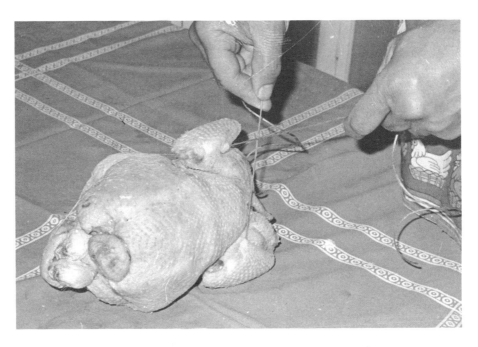

14   Run the string either side of the body and over the wings, pulling the string very tight, and now tie into a knot, cutting off the loose ends.

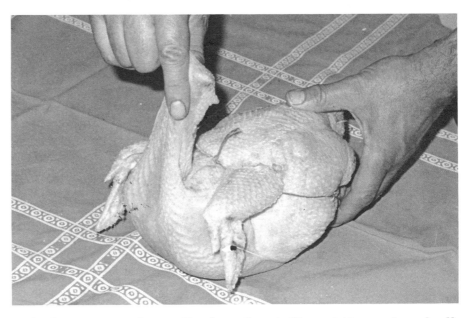

*Step 15.*

15   Pull the loose neck skin up over the knot and fold the wings as shown in the picture on page 112. Turn the bird on its back and you will see that the breast is now raised, looking plump and succulent.

To place the stuffing at the neck end, all that is needed is to pull the neck skin back. Place the stuffing under the skin, replacing the neck skin over the back as before.

*Step 15 (b).*

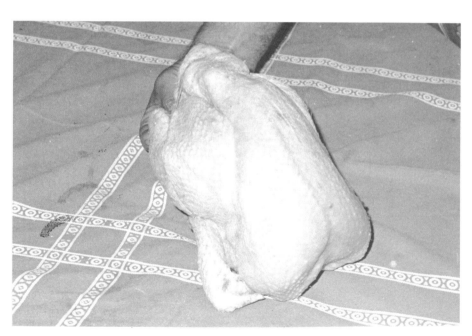

*Step 15 (c).*

16　Now the giblets. The neck has already been separated and placed in a clean dry bowl. Separate the heart by cutting cleanly across the top; now cut away the liver taking care to cut out the gall bladder without rupturing it. If the kidneys have been extracted, these should also be separated. The final organ to cut away from the intestine is the gizzard. Take off any surplus fat and put this in the bowl along with the other giblets. Now carefully slice the thick edge of the gizzard without cutting into the muscular tissue. Having sliced it halfway round the circumference, pull on each side, and in this manner the debris inside the thick skin will stay intact and can be discarded along with the intestines and other waste tissue. As the giblets are cut away, place them with the neck in the bowl. Separate surplus fat from the body, especially that around the inside of the rear opening.

*Step 16.*

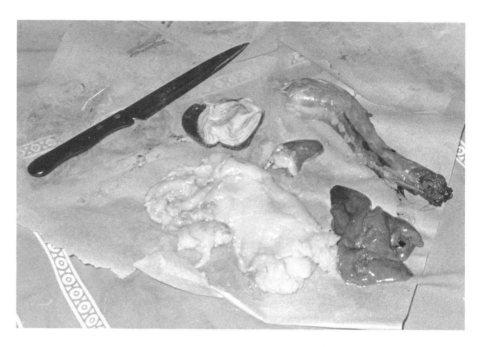

17 All the giblets are now ready to be wrapped up in grease-proof paper, after which they should be put into a small plastic bag.

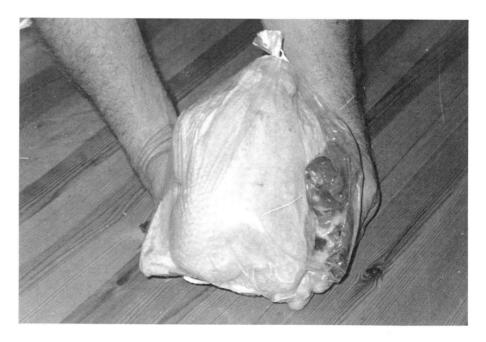

18 Turn the freezer bag inside out and draw over the chicken. Now place the bag of giblets by the side of the chicken and massage all the air out of the bag before tying it securely.

The bile in the gall bladder tastes very bitter and this is why such great care should be taken to avoid breaking it. Many years ago it was customary to wrap up the giblets and put them back inside the carcass. These days, the giblets should be wrapped separately and placed by the side of the eviscerated chicken. The reasons for this are:

(a) The younger generation of customers may not look inside the chicken before cooking it.

(b) The fat may go off if the prepared chicken is kept in a warm refrigerator.

(c) If the giblets have not been thoroughly cleaned there is a risk of cross-infection within the carcass.

Giblets are sold with the chicken to prevent too much weight loss and for the experienced cook to use as stock. Unfortunately, there are those who do not know how to cook them, so they are discarded. By placing the giblets on the outside, they can be handled without having to untie the bird.

Health regulations vary in many countries and even where they are the same, policing by local officials may vary enormously. It is therefore advisable that producers wishing to prepare table birds for resale, seek advice from the local authority before embarking on this type of enterprise.

# 10 Planning, Management and Marketing————

Good costings are only obtained with the benefit of expert management, and from this it is possible to develop a marketing plan. Without accurate throughput and costing figures, it is impossible to work out realistic wholesale and retail prices. Chapters on Breeds, Housing, Equipment, Rearing, Nutrition, Egg Production and Common Ailments will all contribute to the build-up of essential knowledge necessary to give the potential producer an enlightened and practical outlook into the whole business of good management.

It is important that the operation is planned well ahead before setting up, taking into consideration local market requirements. From this information, the overall number of laying birds can be assessed, with flock sizes worked out accordingly.

A sales potential of 176 dozen eggs per week will require a total laying flock of 400 birds. To allow for those coming into lay as flocks are depleted and replenished, the overall flock size will need to be increased to 500 birds. All too often insufficient thought is given to continuity when planning a new enterprise, the newcomer purchasing the total flock number required to produce his total projected weekly retail/wholesale number of eggs in one intake. No thought is given to the fact that customers have their own individual preferences on the grade of eggs they wish to buy. If producers are unable to provide the egg sizes required, customers will look elsewhere for a more reliable source, which may be the farmer's nearest competitor.

With only one intake, when the pullets first commence laying, most eggs will be small or very small. A few customers will buy these for young babies and cooking, but it is a limited market. As the birds become older, egg sizes increase until the bulk of eggs produced are large. When the time comes to deplete the flock at the end of lay, egg production on the farm naturally ceases.

The period of depletion, cleaning out and bringing in new pullets is about four weeks. Then a further three to four weeks must be allowed before any eggs are produced, followed by four more weeks before any real quantity of eggs are laid. The majority of these will be small pullet eggs, and it will take a further three to four months before eggs are of a sufficient size to satisfy the majority of customers. It can therefore be seen that it takes at least three months from depletion before any saleable eggs become available, which is very hard on the cash flow, and makes it even harder to keep existing customers and attract new ones.

It is generally not practical when starting a business from scratch to expect

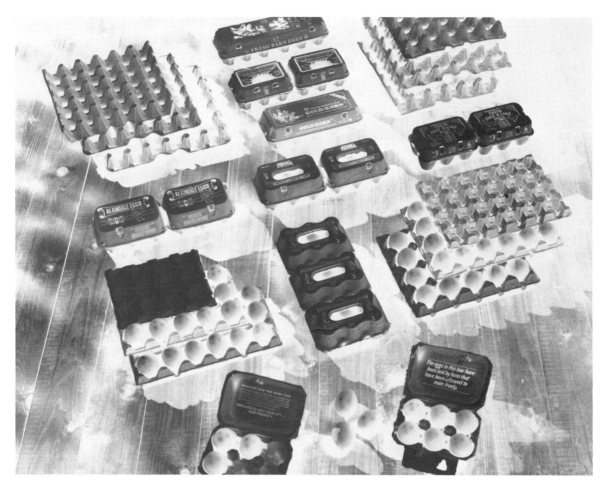

*Keyes trays and pre-packing.*

to obtain predicted total sales at the beginning of the operation, but rather to build them up over the next twelve to fourteen months. The practical solution is to divide 1,000 by four (flocks of 250), and install these on a two-monthly basis. Then add a fifth flock of 250 pullets to maintain continuity of eggs from 1,000 laying hens, the extra 250 covering for flocks as they are depleted and replenished.

The advantage of a series of individual flocks is that they can be increased or decreased according to sales, without having to wait 14 months before such alterations can be effected, as would be the case of one single-aged flock. Only for those producers who cannot be bothered to sell their own eggs (relying on contracting their total output to an egg packing station) can a single flock be justified. By contracting out egg sales, the producer has no control on egg prices, which will fluctuate according to supply and demand. If money has to be borrowed to set up a single-flock venture from which the production is contracted out, then it is doubtful whether packing station returns will be sufficient to repay such loans. Where sales and prices are under the

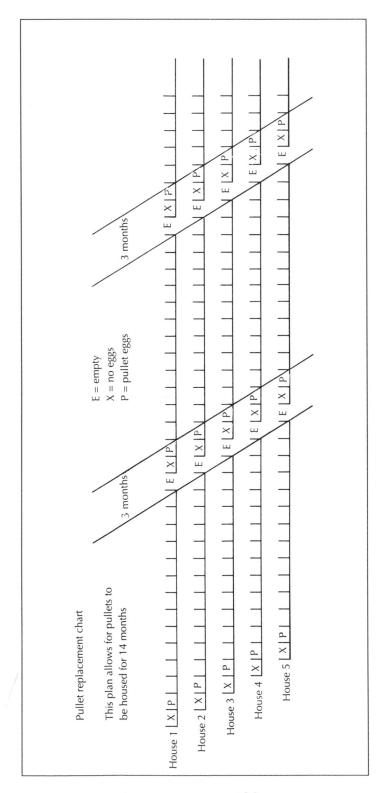

*Pullet replacement chart. This plan allows for pullets to be housed for 14 months.*

owner's control, the creation of a steady weekly demand protects prices by naturally levelling out possible fluctuations, and because of it, a good profit can be achieved.

A mark-up of around 120 per cent is possible by retailing one's own eggs over what can be expected from a packing station egg contract, but allowance should be made for the extra costs of a split unit, being slightly more labour intensive, plus additional costs of advertising, prepacks and delivery where applicable.

Potential free-range egg producers must under no circumstances expect that once the unit has been set up, there will be an unending queue of customers to buy their product, however well produced. The producer has to go out and sell eggs to get new customers. It is hard work and time consuming, but once achieved, is worthwhile and financially very rewarding.

## BIRD SELECTION

Selection of the right bird for free range is very important. The majority of hybrids available have been and are being bred for intensive egg production, and have as such lost many characteristics which are required for outdoor egg production.

Body size is smaller to reduce feed intake without affecting production or egg size. Because of much improved hygiene conditions now experienced by intensively farmed layers, immunity levels have become lower together with reduced density of feathering, etc. Their outdoor counterparts need body size enabling them to consume a greater quantity of feed, to sustain them during extremes of climate without adversely affecting egg numbers. They need a thicker layer of feathers as insulation, and because of the greater risk of cross-infection from the

land and air, their resistance to disease must be greater than that required of their intensively kept sisters.

Where hybrids meant for intensive production are put on range in small units they tend to stand around all day in the house when the weather is cold, wet or windy. This creates boredom, leading to bullying, feather pecking, egg eating and subsequent stress. The producer, in turn, may be affected by higher flock mortality and consequent drops in egg production.

Mammoth-size free range units of several thousand birds, from which only a small percentage of hens venture out, rely on debeaking the hens at an early age to alleviate bullying, which in turn leads to cannibalism. These, and the large barn/perchery units are now the only egg producing systems where birds have to be debeaked. It is also in these mammoth units that panic can be a problem causing further mortality, especially if situated in an area of low-flying aircraft. As has been said in an earlier chapter, flocks of more than 500 birds are subject to increased problems, caused by too few birds venturing out on range. Those that do, pollute the immediate ground surrounding each house unless that area is fitted with slats or gravel.

In the UK at the moment, there seems to be only one hybrid which can withstand and enjoy the changes of the British climate, and are ideally suited to free-range conditions, and that is the Black Rock. There may be other suitable hybrids on offer in the future, but at the moment, from the breeder's point of view, there are insufficient numbers of extensively kept birds to warrant altering their complicated intensive breeding patterns at this point of time.

Free-range layers require different energy rations, lower or higher protein, according to the prevailing climate. It is economical to feed a higher-protein feed during the winter when the bird requires extra for heat and energy. Such rations it is hoped will become more readily available as numbers of layers kept extensively increase.

## AGE AND QUALITY OF STOCK

Where capital is restricted, it is inadvisable to buy day-old-pullet chicks to start an egg-producing unit. To do this requires extra capital for setting up a brooder house and for ancillary equipment. Extra labour may also be required as well as extra feed until the unit becomes functional (in production). All this ties up capital, which could be better invested in the envisaged laying unit which would provide a more immediate cash return.

Where a potential unit is restricted by available land or it is impossible to keep the rearing unit well away from the laying site, the argument that home-reared birds are cheaper than those bought at the point of lay is not always sound. Unless replacement stock is reared professionally at a separate site, there will always be a risk of disease from cross-infection, air-borne or physical contact from mature birds on the same site.

Young pullets reared without light control during late spring and early summer may, as a result of extended hours of light, come into lay too early with an abundance of small eggs, never quite achieving the egg sizes promised in the breed prospectus.

Bought-in eighteen-week-old pullets should be fully vaccinated which is the norm when buying from a reputable supplier. The supplier should be able to offer genuine practical advice before and after birds have been purchased. This is very important, as there is no substitute for sound practical experience.

The extra cost of buying in top-quality birds can be recovered with the extra production they should give. For example, a bird which lays between 6 to 12 extra large eggs over a twelve-month period will more than recover the initial extra cost of the pullet in egg value.

## FEED AND HOUSING

A good-quality feed will assist pullets to produce to their potential in egg numbers and size. When retailing these eggs, apart from considering local opposition, it is important that they are priced to suit the producer's own costings and targeted profit margins. Feed represents some 70 to 75 per cent of the cost of production and is therefore largely responsible for calculating a realistic wholesale and retail price. Additive-free rations should be of a similar price to standard rations, if not the same, but where organic rations are fed the price of the egg must be considerably higher. This is where a good understanding of the local market is essential to ascertain the percentage of customers likely to pay the substantially higher price required for organic production. It must never be assumed that the production of organic free-range eggs is a licence to print money.

Birds will only produce to their maximum potential in well-constructed purpose-built poultry houses. Ventilation must be well thought out to cope with seasonal changes. Forced ventilation will be required in mammoth units to avoid dead spots, and prevent the litter becoming damp, because in these units birds excrete most if not all their faeces in the house. Well-constructed wooden poultry houses, including wood and felt roofs, are all that is required for the smaller unit, i.e. up to 500 layers.

One of the main attractions of home-produced eggs is that they are normally the freshest available. The customer can identify them with the farm where they are produced, more especially if they are able to see the birds and the conditions they are kept in. Attractive poultry houses will give a good impression to those driving by, especially if at least one pen is by the road or entrance. A few producers have on public display a small house and run containing a few different breeds of interest. This provides a topic of conversation and is an attractive draw to children, who will pester their parents to return again and again, especially during the holiday period. If local shops are to be supplied, they must never at any time have their retail prices undercut by those of their supplier at his farm shop. This will result in bad feeling and subsequent loss of local trade. If there is a glut of small pullets' eggs, these can be safely offered at a very cheap price without upsetting the local village shop.

## COSTING

At the beginning, it is very easy to sit down with a calculator or computer, and work out a brilliant set of costings from the various production figures quoted in advertisements and glossy brochures obtained at various poultry shows, or which fall out of innumerable farming and smallholder magazines. It is also misleading to use figures produced from a flock of six to twelve birds which have completed a year's lay. In general, the larger the flock the greater the peck order and associated stress, giving rise to a slightly reduced egg production. This also depends on the stockmanship of the operator. It should be appreciated that it is livestock which are being costed, not deadstock, and with live birds there are many imponderables. Costings and cash

flows unfortunately never seem to work out, and this is the reason why it is so important to keep daily records of egg production, feed consumption, mortality, daily internal and external temperatures plus anything else which may affect performance.

After a while, as recording becomes more established, one is able to start costing the production site and the various laying flocks. Over the next year or so, it will become clearer how the *average* flock performs under each particular environment, including variations experienced with different hybrids and feeds. From this information it is possible to see where feed energy values may be improved, enabling the producer to hold feed consumption at a more cost-effective level during the winter months.

Large individual flocks of birds in the main are liable to produce less eggs per bird than smaller well-managed units. Against this, the cost-effectiveness of labour has to be included in the equation. It is possible that a well-managed individual flock of 100 to 500 layers will be more profitable than equally well-managed individual flocks of over 1,000. The very large mammoth units generally benefit from economy of scale. The most profitable of all egg producers are those who sell direct to the public, the smaller shops, hotels and restaurants. Much, if not all, the labour on a smaller unit is family orientated, so no hefty wage bills have to be paid out each and every week.

It is important that the newcomer does not sink all his or her capital into the enterprise at one go, but gradually builds up on experience which in turn gives confidence to expand as the enterprise progresses. Expansion plans can be plotted and cash flows more accurately worked out, as the necessary practical background information emerges.

## Cutting Costs

A common yet not necessarily effective way to keep initial costs low is to search the market for cheap pullets. Pullets are only cheap if they perform to their potential. A batch of pullets from one rearer costing as much 40p more than another, have only to lay 6 eggs more to recover the extra cost. A saving of £200 on 500 birds may seem at the time a much more attractive proposition, but this saving may easily be eroded by poorer egg production from inferior stock. Pullets supplied by the smaller rearers tend to cost more because of higher overheads. But when reared in smaller units and under the control of one experienced owner-rearer, they have a better chance of producing to their true potential than those reared in flocks of several thousand.

Pullets which are large-flock left-overs (after the main orders have been supplied), are often offered at bargain prices to clear the site quickly for the next batch of chicks, but being the small tail-enders they rarely produce the quantity or quality of eggs budgetted for.

Egg sizes are vitally important, and these are either affected by birds coming into lay too early or from poorly reared birds.

There are many ways to cut costs in rearing, such as using the cheapest brand of feed available, whether it is sufficient to supply the needs of a growing bird or not. To overstock a unit will also reduce overheads as well as selling them a week earlier than that stated, so saving a week's feed and wages, along with other overheads. Each week saved allows more birds to be reared over a given period; the operation is therefore more viable to the rearer and less profitable to the producer.

*New pullets in a slatted floor feeding house with galvanized hanging feeders.*

# MARKETING

Having carried out all that is required up to and including the production of grade A eggs in the most economical manner possible, to complete the operation, good marketing has to be achieved.

A producer is allowed to sell ungraded eggs directly to the public without a Packing Station Licence, provided the farm shop or the owner's house is the only site from which eggs are sold. Once eggs are sold as graded, a Packing Station Licence is required. Only graded eggs are allowed to be sold in shops, and this cannot be done without a licence. Many small producers will grade all their eggs

## LAYING HOUSE RECORD

DATE HOUSED:     AGE AT HOUSING:     NO. HOUSED:     HOUSE:

| Age | Date | EGG COLLECTIONS | | | TOTAL EGGS | Mortality /Removals | No, of BIRDS | FEED | TEMP. Max/Min | REMARKS |
|-----|------|---|---|---|-------|-----------|--------|------|----------|---------|
| | | 1 | 2 | 3 | | | | | | |
| | | | | | | | | | | |
| | | | | | | | | | | |
| | | | | | | | | | | |
| | | | | | | | | | | |
| | | | | | | | | | | |
| | | | | | | | | | | |
| | | | | | | | | | | |
| | | | | | | | | | | |
| | | | | | | | | | | |
| | | | | | | | | | | |
| | | | | | | | | | | |
| | | | | | | | | | | |
| | | | | | | | | | | |
| | | | | | | | | | | |
| | | | | | | | | | | |
| CUM. Total | | | | | | | | | | |

*A laying house record chart.*

for sale to provide an even product. This is allowed provided no grade sizes are displayed or quoted. Grading records provide the producer with necessary additional information from which to compare one flock with another. Recorded egg sizes and numbers are a good indicator of the profitability of each flock. High or low temperatures and type of feed will also affect egg grades. In other words, it is advisable to grade all eggs even when a licence is not required.

To become a registered packing station is not difficult or expensive. Contact an officer of the Egg Inspectorate whose name, address and phone number can be supplied by your local Ministry of Agriculture and Fisheries office. Do this

*This egg grader can sort 1,500 eggs per hour and is suitable for a small packing station or a flock of up to 1,500 birds.*

while you are still in the initial stages of planning, or before your total egg production needs the advantage of shop outlets. An early contact gives the Inspector the chance to meet you and discuss plans and give advice, avoiding unnecessary and expensive problems, as well as keeping on the right side of officialdom.

Setting up a free-range unit without researching possible outlets may result in heavy losses and enforced early retirement. Work must be carried out on assessing potential sales, and from this information the unit can be planned. The EC have made three main regulations which control marketing standards for hen eggs. These are continually changing as they are updated. The legislation defining the various types of production that may be envisaged, such as deep litter, barn/ perchery or free range, will

need to be checked. The area per bird will continue to alter until an equitable solution is arrived at, somewhere between what is required by the laying hen and the viability of a unit as seen through the eyes of 'big business'.

MAFF, together with the Egg Inspectorate, should be able to provide the latest information, especially with regard to egg grades. At the time of publication there is a considerable amount of argument between the large multiples, producers and the EC about redefining egg grades and terminology at point of sale. Whether egg sizes will continue to be classified numerically or revert to the earlier British description of Large, Standard, Medium and Small no one is sure. But whatever the decision, in all probability it will be changed again in the foreseeable future.

# 11   Common Diseases—

'Good stockmen are born not made', so the saying goes. Whatever the case, a good stockman should be able to spot a problem immediately, commencing treatment before the disease or parasites are able to take hold. This may be the difference between the profit or loss of a particular flock, or – should it be serious enough – the poultry farm.

Post-mortems will tell us what a particular bird has died from, providing guidance as to the best way to treat an outbreak, but, unfortunately, the diagnosis may only point to the secondary cause, not the primary problem. It is left up to the producer or advisor, to identify the cause of the problem, and in so doing, adjust management accordingly.

Good hygiene and a daily inspection of flocks is critical. Feed, water consumption and egg production should be recorded, plus any other matter, such as climatic conditions or a fright by animals, children or low-flying aircraft, which may give rise to stress. Some of the problems in this chapter may not occur in a stress-free environment. Such a Utopia is rarely attainable, and because of this, any condition of management leading to stress, however minimal, will need to be attended to.

The first symptoms manifested by laying birds are normally associated with a drop in egg production and appetite. Particular attention should be given to what has taken place three days prior to the drop. Birds cannot just switch off production at will; three days allows for

the cessation of the ovary to come into effect.

When any form of treatment is given, it takes ten days before the true effect becomes evident. If production improves before this time, then it can be safely assumed that it is not the treatment which has brought about this improvement, but that the original diagnosis may not have been correct.

## ASPERGILLOSIS

This is a disease which can easily be avoided by good hygiene. It is caused by inhalation of large numbers of spores from mould. Damp feed which has dried on the floor, dusty hay, straw bales, shavings and the house not being cleaned out properly leaving fungal deposits on the floor, placing chicks or even adult birds on stale dry litter, dirty incubators,etc.

Chicks are the most vulnerable, and mortality can rage from 10 to 50 per cent, depending on how soon or where the infection was picked up. The clinical symptoms appear usually from 1 to 3 weeks of age. Infected birds are stunted and gasp for breath, they are lethargic and have an increased thirst. There is no cure, and all infected chicks should be killed quickly and humanely. The cause must be traced so that later hatchings do not suffer.

Many years ago a batch of 10,000 infected chicks were received from a large hatchery. It was later discovered that the problem had been caused by mouldy mouse poison left in a large walk-in hatcher. The eggs infected were those in direct line to the mouldy poison, spread by the forced ventilation system.

## INFECTIOUS BRONCHITIS

This respiratory infection is now rarely seen in large flocks where young pullets have been vaccinated during the growing period. It is now mainly seen on farms or smallholdings where chicks are bought in at day old, and are not vaccinated during the rearing period. Vaccinated birds can still be infected when the field challenge is greater than the immunity given by the vaccine.

The virus is airborne and also passed from bird to bird via the respiratory tract. Birds that have been infected remain as carriers. Stress can also cause IB to show, such as when new pullets come into lay.

The first sign is a drop in egg production, white-, thin- or crinkley-shelled eggs, or those which have a series of rough ridges around the circumference of the egg. The whites of the eggs become very watery, similar to when birds have been kept too long in lay. Infected birds will have a nasal discharge as well as gasping and sneezing. This is clearly heard in the poultry house after they have perched and settled down for the night. Mortality in young chicks can be as high as 30 per cent but laying birds may not show any increase. The period of this disease lasts for 10 to 14 days, after which time, production will be seen to improve. They rarely ever reach their original peak, and although in general the shell thickness and colour improve, more poor-shelled and cracked eggs are produced from a previously infected flock.

It is advisable, as soon as it is viable, to deplete the flock, thoroughly cleaning out, disinfecting and resting the house for at least 6 weeks. Continue the control, by making sure all future flocks are vaccinated with both live and inactivated (oil-adjuvanted) vaccines.

## NEWCASTLE DISEASE (FOWL PEST)

This is a very infectious disease, and fortunately has not been seen in the UK since the early 1980s. It was brought under control by a Government compulsory vaccination programme, and rigid poultry importation restrictions.

The galvanizing effect of this respiratory infection is unlike any other. Birds reach to the sky while trying to take breath, the droppings are loose and green, but even more important is that the birds showing symptoms one day are all dead the next. Each day mortality doubles that of the previous day.

The Ministry of Agriculture and Fisheries must be notified immediately, and the person/s looking after these birds must not go near other flocks until such times as they are given permission to do so by a Ministry Vet. All birds on the farm have to be killed and burnt or buried. No new flocks are allowed until houses have been thoroughly disinfected with a prescribed disinfectant, and have been kept empty for at least 6 weeks, depending on instructions from the Local Government Veterinary Officer.

## INFECTIOUS BURSAL DISEASE (GUMBORO DISEASE)

In this country it is a relatively modern disease, first recognized in the Gumboro district of Delaware, USA. It is a viral infection which infects the bursal, an internal gland situated at the base of the tail. Mortality is seen in young growing birds, and there is evidence to suggest that some breeds are genetically more resistant than others. Once growers are 18 weeks old, then the danger of infection is passed. The first outbreak I witnessed was in 11-week-old growers; younger birds some distance away were also infected within the next fortnight, even after stringent hygiene conditions had been imposed.

Mortality in a flock lasts for 4 days and then finishes, after which time birds which were off-colour will recover. Affected birds appear ruffled, sometimes shivering, generally unsteady, lose their appetite, and with a watery white discharged from the vent, the feathers surrounding are white and sticky. Mortality ranges from 5 to 30 per cent but in small flocks very rarely higher than about 8 per cent.

Infected birds cannot be treated. On farms where there is a problem, it can be controlled by putting the appropriate vaccine in the water as soon as they are 3 weeks of age, the time when their maternal antibodies are at their lowest.

On farms where rearing is seasonal, there is no need to treat the following year's chicks, but where chicks are reared all the year round, the vaccination programme will have to be adhered to on a continuous basis.

## MAREK'S DISEASE

The expression of Marek's Disease in vaccinated birds can vary, not only from farm to farm, but also from house to house. The time of onset, the severity of the outbreak and the type of lesion seen can vary, too. The reason for this is because one or more of the following are involved:

(a) **The Weight of Field Challenge.** It has been shown that even fairly mildly pathogenic Marek's viruses from serotype 1, if given in sufficient quantity to chickens, can induce severe Marek's lesions. For this reason, it is important to ensure good farm management to reduce the risk of an early challenge from Marek's viruses. The Marek's virus which is excreted through the feather follicles is extremely resistant to environmental conditions. It can therefore be quite difficult to rid a farm totally of Marek's Disease. However, the concentration of that virus is important, and reducing it by thorough disinfection is an important part of disease control.

(b) **The Age of the Bird When Challenged**. The younger the bird, the more likely it is to develop early signs of Marek's Disease. There is a certain degree of age resistance which starts to come into play after about three to four weeks of age, and there is a loose correlation between the age of challenge and the onset of the disease. However, this correlation is not 100 per cent, since the virulence of the virus (i.e. the ability of the virus to cause disease) is also an important part of this equation.

(c) **The Virulence of the Field Virus**. The ability of the virus to cause disease will depend on when the disease occurs, how severe the outbreak is and the type of lesion seen. Normally, the more virulent the virus the more likely the birds are to develop the clinical signs. This appears to be the case with VVMD (Very Virulent Marek's Disease virus), which has been becoming more common throughout the world in recent years. The VVMD is capable of causing visceral tumours (tumours of the internal organs) rather than the classical neuronal tumours (tumours of the nerves). Its symptoms appear as lameness on one leg, with the wing dragging the ground.

137

(d) **Genetic Resistance of the Birds or Breeds**. Genetic resistance has been documented for some years. The recorded evidence shows that certain strains of birds or breeds are more susceptible than others, the light breeds being the worst affected. It is possible to breed Marek's resistance into a strain, and many strains of hybrids and a few pure breeds are showing a very high level of resistance.

(e) **The Level and Type of Maternal Antibody in the Day-Old Chick**. There is still, to some extent, controversy about the role maternal antibodies play in the day-old chick. Where there is evidence of severe disease pressure, it is normally considered good practice to try to alternate the type of vaccine used between different generations of chicken, i.e. alternative years.

(f) **Concurrent Virus and Vaccine**. It is known that there is a balance between the Marek's viruses in the bird. Unlike many other vaccine viruses, the Marek's vaccine virus remains in the bird throughout its life. Similarly, if that bird comes into contact with a field virus, it may become infected by that virus, in which case both the vaccine and the field virus will remain in the bloodstream for life. As a result, there is an even balance between the vaccine and the field virus, preventing the disease from breaking out. The balance is always in favour of a field virus, and should the latter be stronger, then an outbreak of the disease may occur.

If birds are under stress then the clinical signs will be evident. It is important to remember that any disease agent which causes immune suppression can potentially result in Marek's disease, even in vaccinated birds. It is well documented that if birds are suffering from Chicken Anaemia or Gumboro, and are challenged by a virulent Marek's Disease virus, the disease that results will be severe.

Purchasing day-old chicks, whether Marek's vaccinated or not, should an outbreak occur in the growing period, the infection has occured at the rearer's site and not at that of the breeder. Chicks should never be reared near a mature flock but kept completely separate during the growing period. It is appreciated that when chicks are reared under a broody hen, unless a strong field challenge takes place, they rarely go down with the disease. Losses may occur as pullets come into lay, although they have up to that time not shown any clinical symptoms; this can be due to the stress young pullets are under as they commence lay. A high incidence of parasitical worms can, along with other forms of stress, cause the disease to develop.

## COCCIDIOSIS

Coccidiosis is certainly one of the most serious infectious diseases in young poultry. It is most common in very young chickens, although it can appear in older birds (18–25 weeks of age) if they have been reared on a wire-floor system. Such birds are unable to maintain or even increase their immunity levels because they have not been in contact with their faeces. Once these birds are placed in a floor environment such as deep litter or free range, the flock may become infected. It is relatively easy to treat once the problem has been identified, but unless treated immediately, a high mortality may occur and the remaining pullets will rarely lay to their full potential.

Chickens reared in litter are at risk of going down with caecal coccidiosis, the first clinical signs appearing at between 3 and 8 weeks of age. If a coccidiastat is not included in the ration of floor-reared chicks, should an outbreak occur, it will become evident at approximately 3 weeks of age. However, once treated, there should be no further risk of infection for the rest of their lives.

If a chick ration incorporates a coccidiastat, they should be fed this up to 14 weeks of age, that will mean that the grower's ration fed from 8–14 weeks should also contain a coccidiastat. The inclusion of the drug is no guarantee against an outbreak. It is only effective to the level of a standard challenge under good hygienic conditions. The owner has to ensure that all chicks are reared under such conditions, cleaning the whole unit out thoroughly between batches, and not mixing different age groups too early, i.e. not before they are 18 weeks old. When carrying out the daily chores of feeding and watering, these should be done in 'age order', starting from the youngest birds and finishing with the oldest. This will help control any risk of cross-infection. Hands must always be washed between handling birds of different ages. Once birds are old enough to be housed with a grass run – at about 8 weeks of age – only well-rested pens should be used. The coccidiae occysts are always present in the ground, which is reinforced by wild birds. The build-up occurs as soon as a batch of birds are reared over the area, and if not fully rested for 6 to 8 weeks, the following batch may be infected to the extent that the disease becomes clinical.

Coccidiosis is a disease of the intestine caused by a microscopic parasitic organism (protozoon) called coccidia. There are at least eight different types of coccidiosis which occur in chickens, and although some of these types may, under certain conditions, produce severe disease, others are relatively harmless. Coccidia are found in sheep, goats, pigs, calves, and rabbits etc. It is said to be 'host specific' in that the chicken type (e.g. Eimeria Tennella) will not spread to other animal species, including turkeys and ducks.

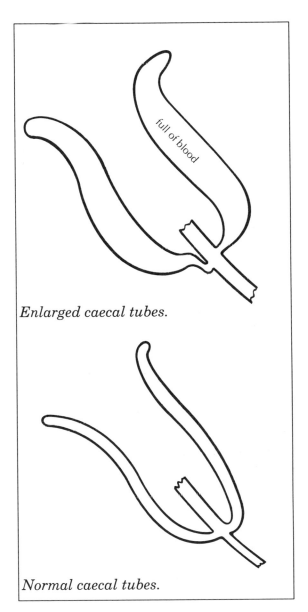

*Enlarged caecal tubes.*

*Normal caecal tubes.*

*Coccidiosis.*

It is found in the caecal tubes, commonly referred to as the blind gut, or in the case of duodenal coccidiosis, in the small intestine, especially in the chronic stage. On opening up infected birds, the caecal tubes are found to be bloated with blood. In duodenal coccidiosis, the small intestine will be very inflamed. Birds stand around hunched with puffed-out dull feathers, their combs very anaemic. When caught, they feel light through loss of weight and are lethargic. Those suffering from caecal coccidiosis can be easily diagnosed by squeezing the abdomen area gently: blood or blood-stained faeces will be excreted.

Unless treated immediately, very severe losses will be incurred. The treatment is only available from the vet. Several infected chicks or young birds should be taken for post-mortem. After confirmation the vet will supply the necessary medicine with appropriate instructions. Once the treatment has been started, a very speedy recovery will ensue, and infected chickens seem to recover overnight. No other losses should occur.

The full course of treatment advised must be strictly adhered to; otherwise the infection may change from the acute to chronic state, the latter being far more difficult to treat, also causing further damage to the gut. During the course of treatment, all birds must be confined to the house, for otherwise they may be able to take on liquid via the eating of grass or moisture from the early morning dew. This extra moisture will dilute the treatment and result in only a partial cure, allowing it to become chronic with continuing losses and further damage to the small intestine, to such an extent that the survivors will be poor uneconomic layers. As soon as the treatment has finished, put a soluble multivitamin in the water for a further 5 days, reducing possible stress to a minimum.

# PARASITIC WORMS

## Roundworms and Tapeworms

The two main types of worm are roundworms and tapeworms. The roundworm is round and smooth and the tapeworm segmented. Birds suffering from a heavy infestation of roundworms, when treated, will excrete bundles of dead worms not unlike shredded wheat. These two types differ from one another in the spread from bird to bird.

### Roundworms

These produce eggs which are laid in the bird's intestines and pass out through the faeces. They then undergo a maturation process lasting a week or more, after which they may be picked up by another bird, hatch in the intestine and here develop to a mature worm.

### Tapeworms

Eggs may also pass out via the droppings or be retained within the rear segments of the worm, which periodically break off and are excreted. These eggs, either free or within the segments, are then eaten by creatures such as snails or beatles. Hatching of these eggs takes place in their host, and a stage known as 'cysticercoid' develops within the body of the intermediate host. Only if the host containing the cysticercus is eaten by another bird will the infestation be transmitted. The eating of egg or segments in another bird's faeces will not develop into parasitical tapeworms.

It is not normal for birds reared or kept in cages to become infected. Birds treated before being introduced to deep litter are unlikely to become infected, unless wild birds are able to come into the poultry house. Birds with access to an outdoor environment are most at risk. It is not uncommon to find these worms in water-

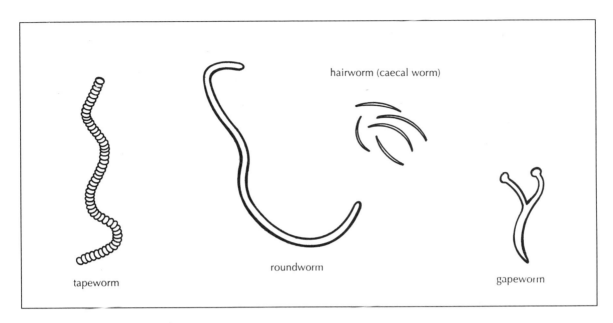

hairworm (caecal worm)

roundworm

tapeworm

gapeworm

*Parasitic worms.*

fowl who love grubbing about and are, in turn, a potential hazard as carriers, when running with hens.

These days, roundworms are the greatest problem, especially where overstocking takes place, or where areas of pasture are never allowed time to rest, so building up the roundworm population to such an extent that new pullets will be immediately affected when put on stale fowl-sick pasture. Pullets, if wormed at 17-18 weeks of age, before putting them out on fresh land, will be able to cope with a gradual build-up of the parasitical worm population, as they mature and their feed intake increases, unless put with older birds on ground not rested, or where birds are continuously stocked at more than 100 birds per 0.4 hectares (1 acre). If there is a continuous stocking rate of 150 birds or more per 0.4 hectares (1 acre) then after the first 9 months, worming will need to be carried out every 3 months. Worming nowadays is normally carried out by the inclusion of the drug in the feed

for 7 days. Eggs produced during this period of worming and 7 days after, must not be sold to the public.

Birds that need worming will maintain or increase their appetite while production decreases. New pullets may start to lay a few eggs and then stop. Their combs look pinkish in colour, rather as if they have been pinched. Unless the outbreak is very severe, no mortality should be experienced. The stress that infested birds suffer may be responsible for an outbreak of Marek's or any other disease which is prevalent at the time. Diarrhoea is also a symptom. Birds suffering from diarrhoea does not necessarily mean that they have worms, unless allied to other symptoms.

## Gapeworms

These are rarely seen in chickens unless they are kept together with infected pheasants, or on infected pasture. The worm invades the trachea (windpipe) causing difficulty in breathing. Infected birds gape for breath, stretching their

141

necks while attempting to increase the aperture of the airway. A long feather with a little oil at the end can be carefully inserted down the windpipe, and, twisting as it is pulled out, will bring with it a few of the worms. The eggs of the gapeworm are eaten by the earthworm in which the larvae are hatched. Birds are infected or reinfected by eating these worms.

The affected flock will need treating immediately with Flubendazole over a period of 7 days. Once treated, the flock should be moved on to fresh ground.

## Hairworms

This worm is not often spoken of, but an infestation will gradually build up on unrested fowl-sick land or pasture. They have a debilitating effect, and if left untreated, birds will die. Like many other stresses, these worms can cause an outbreak of Marek's, especially in young growing birds. They congregate in the blind gut (caeca) and are very difficult to see. If the faeces in this gut is scraped out and mixed in a glass of water, they can be seen and identified.

# EXTERNAL PARASITES

Of the various small biting parasites, the most common are lice and red mite.

## Lice

These do not normally affect egg production but are an irritant to the bird, causing stress, which may set off an outbreak of feather pecking or general bullying, leading to eventual cannibalism. When birds are handled to be inspected, the most obvious signs are a white crustation attached to the base of the feathers around the vent. Where large numbers of lice are involved, these crustations are visible also on the feathers under the wings. They are actually lice eggs. By parting the feathers, small light brown to golden lice may be seen running between the feathers. They bite and feed on skin scales. Their life cycle is on the host and once parted from the host, such as moving on to an animal or human, they do not live very long.

Treatment is either by liberally dousing affected birds with louse powder, or by using a chemical liquid spray, thoroughly wetting the feathers. A weekly treatment of dusting the nestboxes will protect birds from becoming infested, but when cockerels are kept, they need to be treated individually, and on a monthly basis as a precaution.

## Red Mite

An infestation of red mite will cause a drop in egg production, and according to severity, mortality. The life cycle of red mites is not dependent on the host. They live and breed in crevices, as near to their meal as possible. It was at one time thought that they lived only in wood, but they are found living in any material that is adjacent to the bird, including metal. Annual creosoting of the poultry house will prevent the mite from becoming established. There are now alternative sprays which will kill mite but do not remain active over such a long period as creosote.

Apart from causing a drop or cessation in egg production, when entering the house disturbed mite will bite the intruder. A monthly check under each end of the perches will indicate any mite establishment. Only those which have sucked blood will be red; the others are grey in colour. At night they run along the perch, up the chicken's leg and on to the flesh, where they bite into a blood vessel and suck blood until full. They then return to the crevice and stay there until another meal is required. They do not live on the bird so will not be found by examining the bird during the day. Surrounding the crevices is a grey-type ash, which is the mites' faeces. Birds suffering from the presence of large numbers of red mite look pale and jaundiced through loss of blood. A post-mortem shows only a skin which looks as though it has been profusely pricked with a fine needle. Unfortunately, few laboratories recognize the problem, and because of this the owner is left in the dark. Red mite is carried by wild birds and prevailing winds.

New uncreosoted poultry houses are vulnerable, and a good preventative measure is to daub a little creosote in the perch socket with the aid of an old paint brush each time they are cleaned out. There are other mite-killing sprays available to spray the house with; these are normally advertised for pigeons and cage birds. Red mite have been known to lie dormant for up to ten years and for this reason all second-hand poultry houses should be adequately treated before filling with new birds.

## Northern Mite

These mite are said to inhabit the area around the vent feathers. They are similar in size to the red mite but are grey to black in colour, and they live entirely on the host. It is my experience that these mite are more often observed round the head and under the wings. Birds suffering from a heavy infestation tend also to become scabby on the comb, face and wattles. Treatment is by using a spray containing pyrethrum on the affected birds. The mite are difficult to kill and repeated spraying will be necessary.

## Depluming Mite

Where good hygiene is practised this mite is rarely seen, although blamed for bare patches caused by fair wear and tear or feather pecking. They attack the feather shafts, causing the feathers to fall out on the back (rump), neck and head regions. These are also the favourite areas for feather pecking. Treat by spraying as for red and northern mite. Eradication is difficult, and if only a few birds are affected, it would be better to cull these out rather than running the risk of infesting the rest of the flock.

## Scaley Leg

This problem had all but died out, but with the advent of increasing numbers of flocks now kept on range, it is unfortunately on the increase, due to poor management, i.e. not being seen and treated quickly enough to prevent its spread. The mite burrows under the scales of the bird's legs, creating tunnels where it is able to reproduce. As it proliferates, the scales are lifted grotesquely, and if left, eventually makes the bird lame.

This mite is very easy to kill and there are numerous remedies. In the old days, farmers use to dip the bird's legs in old engine oil, suffocating the mite. Vets will probably use an application of a Gamma Benzene Hexachloride emulsion. How long the treatment needs to be repeated depends on how soon it is spotted. When these mite attack feather-legged breeds, it is more difficult to spot, and the owner has to be more vigilant, especially with older birds.

## SOUR CROP (PENDULOUS CROP)

This was at one time more common in turkeys. It is occasionally seen in growing as well as mature birds. The crop is extended and swings as the bird moves. On examination, it is very soft and swishy, and the bird's breath smells sour. It is normally caused by a fungal infection, monilasis or thrush. In most cases it is better to cull the problem bird, but if caught early enough it can be treated with a certain amount of success.

Hold the bird upside-down with one hand gripping both legs. Massage the crop with the free hand, expelling the thick sour liquid out through the mouth. Once the crop is empty, place the bird in a box or cage on its own with only medicated water to drink. A soluble medication such as Vandoline will kill off any fungal infection. After 24 hours, feed with clean whole wheat or mixed corn, and after 48 hours, provided the crop has not started to fill with fluid again, the bird can be put back with the others.

Always keep feeders clean and dry. When feeding wet mash, only sufficient should be put down for the birds to clear up within 10–15 minutes. Stale food must be cleared away and dumped.

## CROP BOUND/IMPACTED CROP

Do not confuse this condition with sour crop. The crop will be similarly distended but feel solid. It does not swing like sour crop, as the distension is caused by pressure of feed pressing against the wall of the crop due to a blockage at the exit of the crop to the glandular stomach. The cause may be eating feathers, litter or long, partially dried grass, which has recently been cut in the poultry run. It can be operated on by a vet, although this will be expensive. It would be less stressful to despatch the bird humanely, after which the crop should be opened to find the cause of the blockage. In this way, having identified the problem, it may be possible to prevent any of the remainder of the flock suffering. If left to its own devices, the bird will die from starvation.

## IMPACTION OF THE GIZZARD

Unfortunately, this is usually caused by poor management procedures. Unless hens are destined for cage production, they should all receive 28g (1oz) per bird per month of poultry grit, starting at a very early age, preferably within the first 4 weeks of their life. Young free-range growers are just as susceptible to gizzard compaction as older birds. Birds given a regular supply of insoluble flint or granite grit will rarely suffer from this problem and are able to make better use of their feed, which can result in the production of a few extra eggs.

## WATER BELLY (DUCKS' DISEASE)

The classic symptom is when a bird starts to walk like a duck, because the abdomen has become so externally swollen that it pushes the legs apart, also weighting the body backwards and off balance. On handling the bird, the swollen abdomen will feel very soft and swishy.

The hen may continue to lay until it becomes too uncomfortable. This problem only affects older birds, and the best layers seem to be more susceptible. There is no known cause for this but it is suspected that the muscles of the older layers have become slack, especially birds which have been the best layers. The stretched muscles allow the body fluids to seep into the body cavity. It could also be that the fluid by-products from the kidneys, which pass through to the large intestine are not recirculated back into the body because of some blockage or degeneration in the intestinal wall but gather in the abdomen.

# INTERNAL LAYER AND EGG PERITONITIS

This has the same visual symptoms as for water belly, but when handled the swollen abdomen will be very hard. It can appear in first-year hens, but is more likely in second- and third-year laying birds. If the abdomen is opened, the hard area will consist of compacted egg yolks. Such a bird is sometimes referred to as an 'internal layer'. This condition is often superimposed by the secondary infection E.Coli, which results in yolks released failing to enter the oviduct, so dropping into the body cavity, where they collect and build up. There is no cure, and affected birds should be culled.

Sometimes a laying bird will for one reason or another drop a yolk into the body cavity. This yolk becomes a foreign body, and because it is now in the wrong place, sets up inflammation of the peritoneum. This is called egg peritonitis. The hen usually dies within twenty-four hours; very few birds ever recover.

The first sign that something is wrong is when the bird stays in the house and stands around the nestbox. Her comb becomes purple and the resultant septicaemia produces a very high body temperature. She will not feed, but if strong enough will perch that night. The following morning she will be found dead under the perch, lying on her side with her neck stretched and curved, the beak pointing to the crop, the comb purple. The bird dies in agony, and this is why, once the symptoms have been clarified, it should be put down immediately to avoid further unnecessary suffering.

There are many possible causes: perches too high, or too little litter on the floor, sudden fright by the operator, dogs, foxes or children.

# PROLAPSE

Rarely seen in intensively kept birds, prolapse is more common when pullets have been range reared during the late spring and early summer, the increased daylight hours causing them to come into lay before they are fully mature. Skilled range rearing by controlling feed intake or protein will help to prevent this from happening, and can be started from twelve weeks of age. It is more common in light breeds, which by their very nature will try to lay too early.

Prolapse happens when the oviduct muscles and vent tissues are not properly developed, or a sudden increase in day length causes too many double-yolked eggs. The vent muscles are pushed out with the egg still gripped inside. On seeing this, pick the bird up and gently break the shell so that the egg can be extracted in smaller pieces, bathe the exposed tissue in mild disinfectant and place the bird in a dark box for the rest of the day. The following day, provide fresh clean water but feed only a little grain, carry on with grain feeding for the next four days, and provided she is looking fit, put her back with the other birds. Do not confuse this condition with vent pecking.

# VENT PECKING

Vent pecking is commonly confused with

prolapse when the owner sees a bird running around or even dead, with some of its gut hanging out. Vent pecking can be avoided under good management conditions. Nestboxes must be placed in the darkest part of the poultry house, and not be a compromise of old trays or drawers. Insufficient nestboxes can also be responsible.

When new birds have started to lay and are reaching their peak, the pullets waiting to lay can be seen walking to and fro along the front of the nestboxes waiting to get in. A hen stands up to lay her egg, and as the egg pushes through the vent, the circular red muscle can be seen surrounding the perimeter of the shell. Red to a hen is an invitation to peck, so when a bystander sees this she will instantly give an inquisitive peck. If blood is drawn, she will be encouraged to continue, so the first bird dies. The following day, she and others will be waiting to peck at any exposed vents and this quickly becomes habit forming. If any eggs are even slightly splattered with blood when collection takes place, the owner should quickly curtain off or make darker the nesting area.

# WET/DRY FEATHER SYNDROME (IMPACTED PREEN GLAND)

This problem is not a disease but it affects ducks and other poultry alike. It is not common, and rarely seen explained in authentic disease books. The preen gland provides the oils to keep the bird's feathers clean and shiny, and in the case of the ducks, waterproof.

The possible causes of this condition are when birds are crowded too tightly together; when they are off colour, which may be associated with insufficient or poor-quality feed; hot and dusty climatic conditions, with little if any water available to bathe in; and in just a very few cases when the gland has become infected with staphylococci or streptococci.

The preen gland, which is situated on the back just in front of the tail, has a sphincter muscle, above which is a thick brush like a tuft of hair, acting as an oil brush when rubbed by the beak. It is this muscle which has become blocked. Once blocked, the preen gland has to be massaged until the blockage is cleared, allowing the natural oils to flow again during preening. Bathe the bird in cool clean water to help stimulate the gland; at the same time this encourages her to preen. In the case of water fowl, it may take several days or weeks before the feathers are sufficiently waterproofed again. Keep a check on the gland during this time to make sure that it hasn't become blocked again. A course of Multivitamins in the water for the next 5–7 days will overcome any stress and bring the bird up to par.

If the preen gland is infected it will look swollen and red. In this case, treatment by a vet with a suitable antibiotic should overcome the problem, although it still may be necessary to manipulate the gland to clear any blockage.

# 12 Preparing Poultry for Exhibition

Many commercially minded poultry breeders and egg producers take a keen interest in breeding birds for exhibition as it is not only a challenge but a very good form of relaxation, provided you have the time to travel at weekends to different parts of the country.

The larger poultry shows take place during the autumn and winter months, but there are also many smaller shows taking place throughout the year, especially at various agricultural shows and country fairs. There may be up to two or three small poultry clubs in each county that meet regularly to hear visiting speakers, exchange ideas and arrange local spring and autumn shows. To take part in this absorbing hobby it is very important to commence with the purchase of quality exhibition stock. After joining a poultry club and attending at least one show, the breed you wish to start with can be selected, but before any decision is made seek advice from those around you. The breeder you buy from should be willing to advise after the sale has taken place.

It is important not to rush into selecting a breed but to observe and find out the problems each breed may pose. There are a few breeds that require pullet-breeding cockerels and cock-breeding cockerels. These are not really suitable material to start with. Select a breed which is attractive to you and simple to breed from. The person you purchase it from will advise, teach and show you how to improve your strain, helping you to progress and eventually win prizes with your own birds.

Keeping a cockerel can cause problems with the neighbours depending on where you live. For those living in a built up area or who have neighbours who will object to the noise first thing in the morning, the cockerel will have to be taken out of the hen house each evening and placed in a large box in the garage or a shed which is relatively sound proof; in the summer time it is advisable to cover over the shed or garage windows keeping the cockerel in complete darkness. A shed is essential when breeding and preparing birds for show, as they need to be kept under cover to prevent the sun and rain from spoiling feather colouration. For example, white feathers will become a yellowish orange colour when kept outside, while brown-feathered birds bleach to a paler brown. The pens inside should be roomy and kept meticulously clean; good ventilation is also important, as are one or two lights to illuminate the shed. If your birds are to be kept in individual pens then the system of giving a pellet feed to keep down dust is acceptable. If birds are to be kept together, then a good coarse grist meal should be fed to avoid bullying and feather pecking. Clean fresh water must be available at all times.

Once you have arrived at the stage where you have one or two potential show birds that have been kept under ideal conditions, you can enter it/them for your first show. It is no good, however clean they look, to expect them to be judged

*Cleaning the scales on the legs with a toothbrush. This prize-winning White Leghorn Bantam was kindly loaned for photographing by Bob Turner.*

unless they have been thoroughly washed and pen trained. Judges will not judge unwashed birds or wild scary ones who, when a judging stick is put through the showpen bars, will try to take off, cage and all, or who will promptly peck or scratch the judges hand as he places it in the pen to withdraw the bird for closer examination.

Training should begin several weeks before the bird/s are intended to be exhibited so they become used to being handled and prodded with a judging stick. Wear a white coat (once they are used to a white coat poultry are not usually worried about strangers in various forms of dress), take your birds out from the pen one at a time, and place them on a table. Do not stand them on a slippery surface but one where they are able to grip with their claws.

Once the bird becomes accustomed to you and is quietly standing still teach it how to stand correctly and proudly by continually correcting its stance with the aid of a judging stick (a 45cm (18in) slim bamboo cane will do). A bird that stands quietly yet proudly in its pen showing off its good points while hiding any faults, will impress most judges, and is already half way there to obtaining an award. As the training sessions progress each bird will become more docile with the frequency of handling so reducing the risk of being frightened when at its first show the judge takes it out of its pen.

Two or three nights before the show each bird entered will need to be thoroughly washed and prepared. Washing is carried out by placing the bird in a bath of comfortably hot very soapy water.

Hold the bird firmly with one hand, positioning the index finger between the legs and gripping them on either side with the thumb and forefinger. Add additional liquid soap with the other hand, working it into the feathers rather like washing your own hair, but take care not to break or bend the strong primary or secondary wing feathers or the tail, and sickle feathers at the side of the tail. Wash the legs, feet and face, gently scrubbing the legs and feet with an old toothbrush. After a thorough washing rinse away all soapsuds by placing the bird in hot clean water; one or two further rinses may be needed until there is no soap left trapped in the feathers. The bird must now be dried as quickly as possible, firstly by using dry, warm towels and then finishing off with a hair dryer. The majority of water can be gently squeezed and ruffled out with the first dry towel and a second will absorb most of the remaining water.

Stand the birds on a towel to blow dry, and follow the simple procedure below:

1. Dry the head and neck first. This makes the bird more comfortable, allowing it to stretch its head up proudly.
2. The second area to concentrate on will depend upon the breed to be shown. If it is a Wyandotte with heavy tail feathers, then it is best to concentrate on the tail area, curving and shaping the tail with the aid of the hair dryer.
3. The wings are the next main area. If a potential show bird has a tendency to droop the primary feathers of the wings, then shaping as they are force

*Drying the head and neck with a hairdryer.*

149

dried will help the bird hold them in a correct position.

Do not hold the dryer too close – use it as if you are drying your own hair. If held too close to the bird the surface feathers will dry too quickly, completely removing all the feathers' natural oils, making many curl unnaturally and stick out awkwardly. The proper use of a dryer helps the owner shape the bird to its best advantage according to the standard requirements of the breed. However expert one becomes there will always be one or two feathers not quite correctly positioned, which is why washing should be carried out two or three days before the show, giving the bird time to re-oil its feathers and look its best.

With the help of a nail file clean out any dirt left under the leg scales and carefully take off any excess beak growth, rather like you would remove an unsightly overgrown fingernail. Do the same with the toenails. Paint the legs and beak with clear nail varnish then immediately wipe it off, leaving a nice shiny appearance. If a bird has a red comb, face and wattles, treat with rouge, also wiping it off immediately. Ensure that the feathers between the eyes and comb are smoothed down, odd ones being plucked out with tweezers. There are many other little tips on preparation but these are individual to each exhibitor and can be picked up at shows or club meetings.

It is the normal practice not to feed birds before judging on the day of the show so it is very important that the night before they receive a good corn feed to help sustain them until after judging. It is also a good idea to give them soluble multi-vitamins in the water two days prior to the show and for five days after. This is because when a bird is moved into another environment it will not eat to capacity for up to three days. The use of soluble multi-vitamins in the water will offset the fall in consumption and keep it in good condition, and a healthy bird is better able to withstand small disease challenges from other show birds, which have been bred and kept in other environments. Birds' disease immunity levels will vary from one to another and a bird suffering from overstress or shock is more likely to succumb than one that is fit and healthy.

It is advisable that the owner brings his own auxilliary supply of corn to the show as well as a suitable container for water should there be any delay in providing a supply after judging has taken place.

After the show, bring the bird home as soon as is practical and place it separately in a pen with an adequate supply of feed and water, returning it back with the other birds when it has finished feeding and drinking. Because there is always a risk of picking up lice or mite at a show, give each bird a thorough dusting with louse powder on its return and before it is put back in with the other birds. A liberal sprinkling of dusting powder in the carrier is also very helpful.

Taking a bird to a show is always stressful, so make sure that all possible measures are taken to alleviate the stress before, during and after the show.

In the UK and in many other countries there is a National Poultry Club. It is worth while considering joining this as well as your local club. The UK secretary is Mike Clark, whose address is:

The Poultry Club of Great Britain
30 Grosvenor Road
Frampton
Boston
Lincolnshire
PE20 1DB

# Glossary

**Addled** A fertile egg in which the embryo has died during the first two weeks.

**Airsac** The air space at the broad end of the egg, denoting by its size whether fresh or stale, and during incubation humidity.

**Ark** An apex-design portable poultry house, usually fitted with a slatted floor.

**Autosexing** A distinct breed of poultry, whose chicks can be identified when hatched by the striping on the down.

**Axial Feather** The short feather between the primary and secondary feathers.

**Barring** The alternative striping of two distinct feather colours.

**Beard** A tuft of throat feathers seen on such breeds as the Faverolle, Sultan and Houdan.

**Bloodspot** Caused by a premature rupture of the small blood vessels in the egg follicle. These appear in the laid egg. Reasons for it may be genetic, nutritional or a sudden fright.

**Boots** Feathers growing down the legs and covering the toes, as with the Brahma and Cochin Breeds.

**Brassy** The yellow tinge in white-feathered birds, seen on the backs and shoulders of those kept extensively.

**Broiler** A young fattening chicken bred for table purposes only.

**Brooder** An artificial heater for rearing young chicks.

**Broody Hen** A laying hen which has ceased lay, sitting tight in the nestbox on any available eggs, with a reduced body temperature. Is used to hatch and rear their own, or imported eggs or chicks.

**Bumblefoot** A swollen foot, possibly caused by a splinter, jumping off a high perch on to a hard surface, or a foot infection.

**Candling** When eggs are put over a strong light during incubation to detect fertility; or when grading eggs for human consumption to detect blood or meat spots, fine shell cracks and freshness.

**Capon** A male bird which has been physically or chemically castrated. Now also refers to a very heavy table bird of 10 to 14 weeks of age.

**Chalazae** Dense coils of albumen attached to the yolk.

**China Eggs** Used to encourage pullets/hens to lay in the nestboxes; also to put under broodies to allow them to settle before placing fertile eggs under.

**Clears** Infertile eggs.

**Cock** A male chicken over 18 months old.

**Cockerel** A young male bird under 18 months of age.

**Comb** The horny muscle which occurs in one form or another on top of the head of most breeds.

**Crest** A crop of feathers over the head of a few breeds such as the Sultan and Houdan.

**Crop** The food collection sac at the base of the neck, it is also the place where food is softened before passing on through the digestive system.

**Cross-Breeding** The mating of two different breeds or two varieties of a breed.

**Cuckoo** A marking of the feathers similar to barring. Where the colours run into one another such as with the Maran.

**Cull** Any unsuitable bird, whether for egg production, fattening or breeding. Stunted in growth, poorly feathered or sickly.

**Culling** To take out any culls from a flock.

**Cushion** *See* **Saddle**.

**Cuticle** Is the final coat put on an egg in the vagina, as a disease barrier before it is laid.

**Day-Old** A chick up to 72 hours old after the hatch is taken from the incubator.

**Dead in Shell** A chick which has died at any stage of incubation. More commonly referred to, but not accurately, as those which have died just prior to hatching.

**Debeaking** The practice of trimming a bird's beak to prevent cannibalism at a later stage (caused by poor management). Has to be carried out on all pullets destined for the large alternative systems, such as the very large free range or barn/perchery environments.

**Deep Litter** A system where birds are kept intensively on litter. Used for growing pullets, broilers and laying hens.

**Down** The covering of hair on newly hatched chicks which is quickly replaced by feathers over the first 5 to 6 weeks of age.

**Dressing** The preparation of a bird for the oven.

**Dual Purpose** Breeds of poultry in the old days suitable for both egg and table meat production. Now widely rejected in most countries, because of the inability to castrate chemically.

**Dust Bath** Normally made by the bird burrowing a hole in the ground or litter, releasing dry soil or litter, to flush through the feathers and partially remove lice and mites. Artificially made boxes of ash or sand are also used.

**Ear Lobe** The flesh immediately below the ears.

**Egg Tooth** The hard horny tip on a newly hatched chick's beak, for chipping out of the shell. Drops off shortly after hatching.

**Endemic** Found regularly in an area or in this case on a farm, such as a disease, etc. Referred to as a disease waiting to become clinical, given the right conditions.

**Evisceration** To eviscerate is to draw out the internal organs of a chicken. An eviscerated bird is one with a hollow carcass.

**Feathered Legs** Feathers which cover the legs to a greater or lesser degree.

**Feather Tracts** Lines of feathers covering the chicken's body.

**Flight Feathers** The large primary feathers on the last half of the wing.

**Fluff** Another term used for the down of a chick.

**Fold Unit** Normally an apex-shaped poultry house and run, joined as one unit to move over an area of ground. To fold. An old system for controlled rearing and breeding. Now more popular as a unit for the garden and orchard.

**Fount** An upright water drinker with an internal barrel, holding a reserve supply of water, controlled by vacuum.

**Free Range** Historically, where no more than 100 birds per 0.4 hectares (1 acre) were kept unrestricted on range. Now a term with many interpretations, relying more on government legislation in various countries.

**Frizzle** A breed of poultry, whose feathers are twisted and turned back in the opposite direction.

**Furnished** A fully feathered bird,

more especially a cockerel with its tail and sickle feathers complete.

**Gizzard**   The muscular internal organ of the chicken, which collects grit eaten by the bird to grind food.

**Grit**   Insoluble granite or flint grit which is fed to birds to enable them to grind their food.

**Gullet**   The feed pipe between the throat and the crop. The oesophagus.

**Hackles**   The long pointed neck feathers and saddle feathers on a cockerel.

**Hardening Off Period**   The gradual weaning of young birds from either artificial heat or a broody hen, over a period of 6 to 8 weeks.

**Heavy Breeds**   A classification of breeds whose ancestry is possibly connected with the Cochin and Brahma, such as the Rhode Island Red and Light Sussex.

**Hen**   A female bird after she has completed her first laying season, approximately over 18 months of age.

**Hock**   The knee joint.

**Hopper**   A feeder with its own reserve of feed above.

**Hover**   An overhead heater directing warmth down by means of a canopy; used for rearing young chicks.

**Hump-Back**   Also called roach-back. A deformity of the back vertebrae creating a lump on the back.

**Hybrid**   A modern term associated with the scientific breeding of commercial poultry. The cross-matching in the laboratory of genetics by blood sampling of grandparent stock.

**In-Breeding**   Mating closely related individual breeding stock such as father to daughter, son to mother/sister.

**Incubator**   A unit to incubate and hatch eggs artificially.

**Intensive System**   A system in which all birds are confined in a poultry house, such as deep litter or barn/perchery.

**Keel**   The bird's breast bone.

**Keyes Trays**   Papier mâché trays used to collect and store eggs on.

**Kibbled**   Corn or wheat split into smaller pieces for young growing birds. Usually maize (corn) is kibbled for mixing with wheat.

**Lacing**   An attractive stripe of a different colour which runs around the edge of the feather.

**Light Breed**   A breed of birds, which are light and quick feathering, more adaptable to hot climates than heavy breeds are. Prone to panic.

**Line Breeding**   Breeding within the family line, without in-breeding.

**Litter**   Material such as wood shavings, wheat straw or shredded paper used to cover the floor of a poultry house. Its purpose is to absorb faeces, provide a dust-bathing and scratching area, and a moderate form of insulation.

**Mash**   A mixture of coarsely ground feed; can be fed dry or wet.

**Mealy**   Describes a defect in the plumage, especially of buff coloured breeds, in which the feathers are more or less speckled with white.

**Meat Spots**   Foreign matter which has broken away from the ovary, and passes down in to the oviduct, to be found later inside the egg.

**Mottled**   A white tip at the end of feathers, as in the Anconas.

**Moult**   The annual shedding of feathers, to be replaced with new for the next season. Takes between 2 to 3 months to accomplish.

**Muffled**   The muff and beard feathers on the side of the face, as in Faverolles, Sultans and Houdans.

**Nest Egg** Otherwise called a pot egg, and used for the same purposes.

**Oesophagus** More commonly known as the gullet.

**Out-Breeding** The mating of different strains of the same breed.

**Pair** One of each sex.

**Pellet** Mash ground very finely and pelleted with a bonding agent such as clay.

**Pencilling** Small stripes in the feather which either run round the edge of the feather or across.

**Petit Poussin** A very small chicken killed for table between 4 to 6 weeks of age.

**Pin Feathers** The new feathers emerging at the time of moult.

**Point of Lay Pullet** A young pullet sold generally between 17 to 18 weeks of age. It does not denote a bird that is going to lay the following day, but within the next 3 to 4 weeks.

**Pot Eggs** The same as china or nest eggs.

**Primaries** The ten large feathers between the wing tip and the centre of the wing.

**Pullet Bred** Birds bred from pullets.

**Pure Breed** Breeds kept pure, not crossed with other breeds or varieties of the same breed.

**Recessive** Recessive characters are those which are suppressed in the first generation, but may show in following generations.

**Roach-Back** The same as hump-back.

**Rose Comb** A broad flat comb covered with small nodules.

**Saddle** The area of the back in front of the tail. Called the cushion in females.

**Scales** These are the horny tissues which cover the legs and toes.

**Self Colour** The plumage of bird or breed which is all one colour.

**Semi-Intensive** Where birds have access to a fenced run or fold. They are restricted within a given area.

**Shaft** The stem or base of the feather.

**Shank** The part of the leg between the hock and the foot.

**Sickles** The long curved feathers of the cockerel's tail.

**Single Comb** A flat vertical comb with serrations along the edge.

**Sitting** A number of eggs for one hen to cover, approximately 12 to 14 for the larger heavy breeds.

**Split Wing** A deformity of the wing where the joining axial feather is missing. Such birds should not be bred from.

**Spur** The horny sharp growth on the inside of the bird's leg. Mainly on the male bird.

**Squirrel Tail** Where the tail feathers grow towards the neck, as the name implies. Can be a fault in Rhode Island Reds, Sussex and many other heavy breeds. Should not be bred from.

**Strain** A group or flock of birds bred from one family line. Individual to the breeder.

**Stubbing** After plucking has taken place, the remaining stubs, quills or base feathers to be extracted, called stubbing.

**Tail Feathers** The stiff upright feathers of the tail, with the exception of breeds such as the Cochin, Brahma and Buff Orpington.

**Taint** Eggs which have been affected by strong smells in the immediate vicinity, affecting the flavour, e.g. stale food, dirty nestboxes, stored with fish or onions, etc.

**Toe-Punching** A system of marking day-old chicks for identification purposes. Putting one or more holes through the web of the foot.

**Trio** The term given to 3 birds, one of which is a male.

**Trussing**   Tying up the carcass of a bird after plucking and evisceration (gutting), for the table.

**Type**   Birds with the correct conformation for their specific breed.

**Utility**   Poultry bred for egg production or meat, not for show or exhibition.

**Variety**   Birds of the same breed but are different in colour, such as Light Sussex and Speckled Sussex. The body shape remains that of the specific breed.

**Vent**   The orifice at the rear end of the bird from which eggs are passed out, and excreta ejected.

**Wattles**   The   fleshy   appendages hanging either side of the lower beak. Should always be even in length with each other.

**Weathering**   The bleaching of coloured breeds and yellow colouring of white breeds, on all birds exposed to the elements, such as those which are kept extensively or semi-intensively.

**Web of Feather**   The barbs of feathers on each side of the central shaft.

**Wing Clipping**   Where the primary and secondary feathers are clipped on one wing to prevent the bird/s from flying.

**Wry Tail**   A tail which leans to the left or right of centre. The bird appear unbalanced. Normally a genetic deformity, but can be caused by damage to the tail in the growing stages.

# Index————————————